More than Human

Making with the Living World

Edited by Justin McGuirk

the Design Museum

MORE

THAN

HUMAN

Solange Pessoa, *Untitled*, from the *Sonhíferas* (Dreamers) series, 2023

Foreword

In 2021, the Design Museum staged *Waste Age*, an exhibition exploring the all-pervasive problem of an economy that depends on disposability and waste materials. It asked the fundamental question: what can design do? The exhibition also launched a partnership between the museum and the Arts and Humanities Research Council and established Future Observatory as a national research programme for the green transition.

Over the last four years, Future Observatory has been at the forefront of commissioning design research focused on reducing carbon emissions, pollution and waste, using the Design Museum as a forum to engage the public in that research. Design has a crucial role to play in addressing these urgent issues. But it has become clear that there is also a need for a fundamental change in how we view the world around us, and our place in the ecosystems that facilitate the life of planet Earth.

More than Human is our challenging response, perhaps the most radical exhibition the Design Museum has ever staged. It reflects a growing desire to shift our collective mindset, which considers humankind to be at the centre of everything, towards a capacity to view the world from non-human perspectives. It resets the overarching narrative of our relationship to the living world – the more-than-human-world.

The exhibition is emphatically multidisciplinary, featuring more than fifty designers, architects, artists and filmmakers, and I would like to thank all of them for taking part and for the ways in which they have begun to rethink their creative practices. I would also like to thank the curatorial team led by Rebecca Lewin at the Design Museum and the director of Future Observatory, Justin McGuirk, who devised and shaped the idea of *More than Human* from the outset. In editing this book, he has assembled a group of writers and thinkers who are helping to formulate a discourse in the early days of an emerging paradigm. Thanks are due to Jennifer Cunningham for her editorial assistance. Finally, I would like to salute the collaborative culture and support of the Arts and Humanities Research Council, which has established a partnership unlike any other in the museum sector, and which I hope is as inspired by *More than Human* as we are at the Design Museum.

Tim Marlow

Introduction

'We' are not the only kind of *we*.
Eduardo Kohn, *How Forests Think*

The irony of calling our age the 'Anthropocene' is that, in acknowledging the awesome power of humans, we place ourselves at the centre of things just when we should be doing the opposite. Yes, we have proven our capacity to change the climate. But do we undo global warming and ecocide by doubling down on our heroic ingenuity, by speeding up the technofixes, or by returning some agency to the living systems that sustain us?

This is a fundamental question for design. There is a great deal of thought and care going into the limiting of human impact on the planet. For decades now, designers have promoted recycling, reuse, repair, low-carbon materials, biomaterials, zero-waste solutions, net-zero construction and other sustainable initiatives – all of which remain essential and ever more urgent. But let's be clear that in most cases such efforts amount to a form of damage limitation, the shaving off of carbon emissions, plastic and pollution by tiny increments. As planetary warming targets recede in the rearview mirror, does it not feel as though we need a shift in narrative? What if we were to frame the entire problem differently? Rather than asking how we reduce our impact, what if we asked how we can design *for* the flourishing of natural ecosystems and other species?

The very act of asking that question requires a shift in perspective. Rather than viewing the world exclusively through the lens of human needs and desires, it requires us to think about what other species need to thrive. The question demands a transition from a human-centric worldview to one that acknowledges that we live in a world that is *more than human*. Anthropologists have been grappling with the implications of this shift in perspective for at least two decades. Only recently, however, has the concept of the more than human begun to take root in design. A new generation of designers and architects is emerging who are forging alternative forms of practice that break away from consumerist models and seek to reframe our relationship with non-humans.

The term 'more than human' was introduced by the ecologist and philosopher David Abram in his 1996 book *The Spell of the Sensuous*. Reflecting on it nearly 30 years later, Abram writes: 'The phrase was intended, first and foremost, to indicate that the realm of humankind (with our culture and technology) is a subset within a larger set – that the *human world* is necessarily embedded within, permeated by, and indeed dependent upon the *more-than-human world* that exceeds it.'[1] Despite being a rather clunky composite, the phrase appears to have stuck. That may be because, unlike words like 'nature' or 'environment', there is no way of saying it without repositioning humans in the order of things. Sometimes the phrase 'more than human' is used to allude to the world of our own technologies, such as AI, which give the impression of having their own agency. But that was not Abram's intention, and nor is it ours in this book. Rather, the phrase seeks to weave humans back into the infinitely complex tapestry of the living world. It is, above all, an appeal to humility, a word that Abram notes shares the same root as human and humus, the very stuff of the earth.

To invoke the more-than-human world is to acknowledge that humans are not the only worldbuilders. Non-humans – from worms to bees, microbes to fungi, trees to otters – create the ecosystems that feed us and the very atmosphere that we breathe. As Darwin noted in 1881, 'Worms have played a more important part in the history of the world than most persons would at first assume'.[2] Acknowledging the millions of 'small agencies' that have made the planet habitable is also, inevitably, to recognise the ways in which human activity has disrupted that agency – from intensive agriculture to infrastructure such as dams, to chemical fertilisers, monocultures and microplastics.

We know that raising awareness of the catalogue of landscape despoliation, biodiversity loss and species decline has not been enough to halt it. We know that the mantra of 'sustainability' has not been enough either. The potential of more-than-human design is that it radically reframes the issue by prioritising not human needs but the living world we depend on. What does it mean to design not just for ourselves but for other species and for the health of natural systems? As a discipline, design is still only in the infant stage of knowing the answer to that question. More-than-human design is a nascent, still in many ways theoretical, form of practice. It is difficult to point to. There are no more-than-human laptops or toothbrushes. It is too soon to expect 'solutions'. But, as an outlook, more-than-human thinking has the potential not just to reframe design's role in the world but to generate something much more fundamental: a liveable future based on our coexistence and collaboration with other species.

The Natural Contract

At the root of all climate and ecological crises is the idea that humans are separate from nature. Human exceptionalism, based on the notion that we are the supreme intelligence on Earth, has been deeply internalised, at least in Western thought. It is at the core of the Judaeo-Christian tradition, and the biblical notion that we have dominion 'over all the earth, and over every creeping thing'. Human-centrism was a tenet of Enlightenment science and philosophy, with its critical distinctions between nature and culture, rational and irrational. The history of modernity, which is one of human progress through technology, can equally be framed as the freeing of the majority of humanity from a direct dependency on the land through industrialisation and urbanisation. Never mind other non-Western cosmologies or Indigenous belief systems that view human civilisation as deeply entwined with the living world: in the modern project, the damage to ecosystems through extraction and pollution was simply an externality – a necessary evil – in the name of development and progress.

Design has been a crucial force in the delivery of modernity. It is a fundamentally human-centric discipline. Indeed, we uphold human-centred design as a mark of quality, as an aspiration. In software and interaction design, for instance, designing for the ease of the 'user' was seen as a significant step away from the kind of engineering thinking that privileged the logic of the machine or system.

So does more-than-human design – which proposes not to put the human first – challenge the very definition of design as we understand it? In some ways it does. But that is not to dispense with the essential humanism of design, and all that is has achieved in making life more liveable for people. Rather, the challenge that more-than-human design presents is how to move beyond that obsession with human comfort, which has come at the expense of so many other species.

In his book *The Natural Contract*, Michel Serres pointed out that the achievements of the Enlightenment came at a significant cost. Thomas Paine's *The Rights of Man* and Jean-Jacques Rousseau's *The Social Contract* had established the equality of men in the eyes of the law, but they left out the rights of the natural world. He argued that, as well as a social contract, we need a natural contract based on 'symbiosis and reciprocity'. For Serres, this required a complete repositioning of humans' place in the world. This position is reinforced by the word 'environment' – that which is around us – a word that places humans at the centre of the natural world. 'Thus,' he writes, 'we must indeed place things in the center and us at the periphery'.[3]

While Serres takes a provocatively radical stance, the extent to which humans are dependent on natural systems has always been understood by ecologists and has been a central tenet of the environmental movement since at least the 1960s. Today, we talk about being 'entangled' in those systems. And while that entanglement has become a cliché, it remains a useful metaphor for the complexity of the web of life. It has been deeply encouraging in recent years to see emerging designers abandon the canonical preoccupations of design (more products, more buildings) to explore that complexity. They may be thinking about the health of the soil, the role of fungi in forest ecosystems, supporting the diversity of urban wildlife, restoring coral reefs, studying traditional forms of land-use or indeed Indigenous ways of living in harmony with the land. They will be working with ecologists, anthropologists and natural scientists, breaking down the disciplinary boundaries between man-made and worm-made, between modern and ancient, between culture and nature.

Making-with the living world

In dissolving the boundaries between 'human' and 'nature', one of the examples that I have found instructive is the basket-weaving of the Ye'kuana people of the Venezuelan Amazon. The Ye'kuana are renowned for their basketry, which is considered an essential skill for all members of society, and is imbued not just with tremendous craftsmanship but with a cosmology based on the animate life of the rainforest. While the Ye'kuana consider their baskets 'culture', they become so not by being fashioned with their own hands, but by requesting the forest's permission to use its materials. This is granted through ritual and song, and only then can a basket be woven. The result is that the basket is sacred, essentially an extension of the forest, and distinct from any of the industrially manufactured objects they may have acquired elsewhere. The basket, in other words, is imbued with the spirit of the forest and is still in some form 'nature'.

Some might categorise this practice as mere superstition or, at best, a considerate form of extractivism. A better way of thinking about it is as a form of coexistence with an ecosystem and a profound acknowledgement of the source of all life and craft. Baskets, the symbol of Ye'kuana culture, are a form of design that is collaborative with the living world.

The theorist Donna Haraway might call this approach to basket-weaving 'sympoiesis', which simply means 'making-with'. One of the ways Haraway has challenged human-centrism is by defining human history as a process of becoming-with all of the countless species that we have coexisted with and depended on. In this, she is building on the work of evolutionary biologists such as Lynn Margulis, who established that species evolve not just through competition, as Darwin thought, but also through mutual cooperation, or symbiosis. By the same token, making-with is an entreaty to make in a way that is engaged with other living beings.

Haraway herself is rarely specific about what that might look like. Contemporary designers, on the other hand, provide any number of examples. It might be designing modular frameworks that enable coral reefs to regenerate themselves; it might be designing architectural facade systems that can play host to insect- or bird-life; it might be designing 'living' breakwaters using millions of oysters to prevent flooding and clean the waters off Staten Island. Indeed, it might mean designing policy in ways such that other species are represented in the decision-making process. In its most literal form, it might mean designing products *with* living materials such as bacteria, mycelium or algae. Here, the designer inevitably cedes some agency to the material, opening up the process to uncertain outcomes and relinquishing control over the final form or finish. Making-with is always, by definition, relational. It is a negotiation, or perhaps even a form of diplomacy. It is situated in the living world in a way that weaves together the human and the non-human. This creative commingling with other species is a form of seeking out, to use Margulis's lovely phrase, the 'intimacy of strangers'.

The question is, how much do we need to understand these strangers to make worlds with them? The possibility of understanding other species at all has been a fraught topic in philosophy ever since Jakob von Uexküll first considered the *Umwelt*, or surround-world, of ticks at the turn of the twentieth century. In the 1970s, the philosopher Thomas Nagel asked 'What is it like to a be a bat?', concluding that we cannot know. But for designers, as for biologists, some shift in perspective is required. How can we design for the benefit of other species without at least knowing the conditions that enable them to thrive? A number of contemporary designers – including Alexandra Daisy Ginsberg, Dunne & Raby and Thomas Thwaites – have explored the perceptions and surround-worlds of non-humans. And while all are only too aware of the limitations of their endeavours, their work is a productive step towards the decentring of the human. This is about more than the cultivation of empathy. Such work requires collaboration with

Weaving a Ye'kuana basket

natural scientists and ecologists in ways that constructively break down the disciplinary boundaries of design. For design, by definition, has been established in opposition to nature. If nature in the Western worldview is 'that which is separable from human activity', then more-than-human design is one way to bridge that seemingly unbridgeable gap.[4]

Design in a minor key
Considering the *umwelten* of other species – indeed, considering other species at all – might be seen as debilitating for designers. The designer is rarely in control of the full life cycle of a product, with all of the damage to other species that ensues from its associated extraction, production and disposal. So to what extent is more-than-human design a *disabling* form of practice, and to what extent is it *enabling*? Or, what old ways of

15

thinking does it close down and what new ways does it open up? If the designer were a Jain, who tolerates no harm to even the tiniest insect, it would be difficult to manufacture or build anything in good conscience. Does that mean we build nothing, or that we consign ourselves to endless hypocrisy? The anthropologist Eduardo Kohn is instructive on this point. In *How Forests Think*, he describes the deep spiritual connections that the Runa peoples of the Amazon possess with the animals of the forest, even embodying them in their dreams. '[T]rans-species interactions depend on the capacity to recognise the selfhood of other beings', he writes.[5] But this does not mean that the Runa do not hunt – rather, it is what makes them good hunters. Like the Ye'kuana, who ask permission to cut their weaving materials, that acknowledgement of the animate life of the forest is what binds the Runa into the web of relations, and keeps their ecology in balance.

Such more-than-human, or beyond-the-human, anthropology has much to offer design. Recognising the lifeworlds of other species is a critical part of that shift in perspective discussed earlier. And observing the role that even the humblest of species play in an ecosystem is crucial to attuning ourselves to it. That is certainly the message that another anthropologist, Anna Lowenhaupt Tsing, has for designers. She often describes her practice as one of 'noticing'. Noticing the way the matsutake mushroom thrived in forests that had been damaged by fire or logging, and the economies that surround the matsutake, offered a clue to what she calls the 'arts of living on a damaged planet'. As she says later in this book: 'Noticing is my way of opposing a particular modernist practice of looking towards an imagined future'. Such futures, driven by confidence in our own technological prowess, always overlook the side effects. These might be the unintended consequences of imperial and industrial infrastructures such as plantations, canals or seawalls, which throw local ecosystems out of balance. Monocultures such as plantations are breeding grounds for pathogens and destructive fungi. Tsing calls these consequences 'feral effects', and she is clear that designers need to get better at anticipating the feral effects of their projects and masterplans.

Where does this leave design? As a discipline, at least in its modernist incarnation, design is a heroic mode of being – designers are tasked with *solutions*, they intervene with *proposals*. A form of design that is inherently cautious, based on noticing and anticipation, requires a shift in mindset. If designers are used to occupying centre stage, it is time to acknowledge that there is no centre anymore, but an infinite number of entangled stages. The philosopher Isabelle Stengers calls this 'escaping the major key'. As she explains, 'there is no form of practice independent of its environment', and we can infer from that that designers, architects and civil engineers ought to be thinking with the particularities of an ecosystem.[6] Design in a *minor key*, then, means dispensing with the heroism and cultivating a radical hesitancy. It may mean thinking twice before acting or, indeed, not acting at all.

If that sounds passive or defeatist, it is not. Rather, design in a minor key is an entreaty to put in the slow work of noticing before rushing in with solutions. It means truly understanding the particularities of a place, and the life that resides there. One of the hallmarks of modernity has been the desire to apply standardised solutions, be it concrete infrastructures, universal plastic everything, monocultures, repetition, repetition, repetition. It is in challenging the efficiency drive that the true political content of more-than-human design may lie. In not just slowing down the gears of business-as-usual development but proposing alternative approaches that respect the living world. Call it 'more-than-human', call it 'regenerative', or just call it coexistence.

Justin McGuirk

1. David Abram, 'On the Origin of the Phrase More-Than-Human', in César Rodríguez-Garavito (ed.), *More Than Human Rights: An Ecology of Law, Thought and Narrative for Earthly Flourishing* (New York: NYU Law, 2024), 3–4.
2. Charles Darwin, *From Formation of Vegetable Mould through the Actions of Worms with Observations on Their Habitats* (1881), quoted in Jane Bennet, *Vibrant Matter: A Political Ecology of Things* (Durham, North Carolina: Duke University Press, 2010), 95.
3. Michel Serres, *The Natural Contract* (Ann Arbor, Michigan: University of Michigan Press, 1995), 33.
4. Donna Haraway uses this phrase in 'Tools for multispecies futures', in *Journal of Design and Science*, October 2019.
5. Eduardo Kohn, *How Forests Think* (Berkeley, California: University of California Press, 2013), 116.
6. Isabelle Stengers, 'Introductory notes on an ecology of practices', in *Cultural Studies Review*, March 2005, 187.

I

Being Landscape

Jojo basket by Ye'kuana weaver Emanejewa, 2020–23

The idea that humans are separate from nature is at the root of all environmental destruction. According to this logic, landscapes are a resource from which we can extract what we need – and a place to dump what we don't – regardless of the consequences. If the Enlightenment placed human reason above nature, mass industrialisation and urbanisation have only deepened our disconnection from the ecosystems upon which we depend.

Can we relearn the ways in which we humans are entangled in living systems? Can we rediscover the natural rhythms and cycles that once governed earlier ways of life? And what is the role of design? The writer Daisy Hildyard suggests that the designer has 'washed up alone in modernity'. In her essay for this chapter, she considers the ways that language and storytelling can build connections to the landscapes that modernity has distanced from us. Likewise, the anthropologist Anna Tsing makes a case for noticing the subtle particularities of an ecosystem, warning designers against the feral effects of standardised solutions.

The artists and designers represented in this section are all in some way seeking to dissolve the division between the human and non-human. Trees become maps, people become trees, calendars become landscapes. There are many approaches by a diverse set of practitioners: some advocate for the rights of rivers, others for the knowledge of forests. Indigenous weavers claim their baskets are nature, while forensic architects argue that the wilderness is actually man-made. The ways in which human activity and the living world are woven through each other are too intricate to be unravelled. As the artists and designers here intuit, we do not merely inhabit landscape, we are landscape.

Justin McGuirk

To feel yourself a landscape

Daisy Hildyard

All human bodies, given time, will eventually become earth. When a long-buried body is discovered, perfectly preserved, inside a peat bog or a melting glacier, there is something disturbing in the fact that it has not returned (through burial, or decomposition, or fire) to the environment. These bodies become stories. Here we have a man who had black tattoos on his abdomen, who often took long walks, who had recently recovered from a bout of sickness. He could be found with his small copper axe and his birch baskets beside him, sitting in a conifer forest on the slopes, eating a picnic of red deer meat and herb bread, some 5,000 years and eight hours ago.[1]

A human body that has not merged with the earth is, among other things, newsworthy. The outlier exposes the norm: that the body belongs to the landscape is an ancient truth. It exists in the material movements of particles via energy, transformation, growth and entropy. It also exists in image, dream, narrative and song. Around the world, across time, people have told stories of bodies that turn into trees, animals, rocks, islands, lakes...the story itself is always moving on and changing shape. We can see it take form in the 'Being Landscape' section of *More than Human* – in the *rumii*, men who are also trees; in Jonathan Baldock's corn dolly masks that are made of bronze: part vegetable, part mineral, part person; in Solange Pessoa's black-and-white paintings of mobile beings whose locks of hair roll into limbs into long toes into manes into webbed hands into coiled bodies into long tails.

These very different works unfold as a cosmic version of the game called Exquisite Corpse, or Consequences, that has been playing out since before the Big Bang. They embody the reality that the human and the landscape are not separate but inset and porous, moving in and out of one another all the time. We eat food, tend plants, care for other species, walk paths into the ground, breathe the air into our bodies; expire. We carry parasites in our bellies and bugs in our hair. Even within the designed and apparently denatured lives of urban modernity, the environment is also already inside. Grains of rice move through the intestine; a wasp is trapped in the bedroom; the microbiome migrates from the swiping fingertip to the black mirror. At an expanded scale, our bodies express themselves, across the planet, via import and extraction, consumption and emission. Daily life depends on the intercontinental movement of crude oil and coffee beans. People wash, cook, work; gases disperse in the atmosphere, waste water is piped away.

John Latham, Ornithological study from The Royal Society of the pheasant-tailed jacana (Hydrophasianus chirurgus), 1787

All this is intuitive, because the connection between the person and the landscape is common sense. Many of the works on show in 'Being Landscape' have this quality of plain utility – a map, a staff, a basket. Marcus Coates's *Nature Calendar* is a simple, sensible work of art: short observations of the plants, animals, birds and environment, noted down each day, through one year. It's a project that many humans must have undertaken, in different times and places, since our life as a species began.

The fact of its exhibition in a gallery is also a mark that this calendar is a rare object now. In the news, in our stories, in conversation, it has often been said in recent years that there has been a breakdown in the relationship between the modern human and the natural world – the live awareness of plants, animals, birds and environment has weakened. This breakdown extends across scales, from private anxiety to global crisis. Meanwhile, those in power attempt – increasingly chaotically – to enforce business as usual. The problem runs on in the background, effectively ignored, like a muted chat.

Historically, the initiation of a separation of person from environment can be traced back through the programmes of colonial modernity – founded in Europe, then spreading around the planet, and still affecting lives globally today. In England, in the seventeenth century, the institution of the Royal Society set the terms for an establishment science that could take for granted a firm distinction between Man and Nature. Early Fellows, their correspondents and role models – from Leibniz to Descartes to the Society's father figure, Elizabethan courtier Sir Francis Bacon – notoriously applied the language of hunting, torture and rape to the study of Nature, who was habitually personified as a woman (and, occasionally, in her uncontrollable promiscuity, as a prostitute).[2] The authors assume a god-like position, above and outside the subjected world.

The Society's work was entwined with that of the colonialist East India Company, founded in 1600. Proto-colonialism and proto-science fed one another.[3] The Society's scientific and technological advances facilitated expansionist trade and conquest; and white voyagers sent accounts of their travels back to the Society: notes on the people they encountered and their tools, beliefs, habits, homes. Samples of plants and minerals were taken and dispatched to London. These activities assume a state of exemption for certain human bodies – a situation in which systemic harm or extraction can be rolled out across the world without consequence to their designers.

Where does all this leave the designer now? One response that comes to mind is: lonely. Washed up alone in modernity, cut off from the rest of the living world. Author and ecologist Robin Wall Kimmerer, a member of the Potawatomi Nation, has written on how this separation is embedded in the English language, which apprehends elements of landscape as nouns: a forest, a river, a hill, a bay. Kimmerer considers how this affects comprehension: 'bay is a noun only if water is dead. When bay is a noun, it is defined by humans.' She contrasts this with the Native American Ojibwe verb for the same marine phenomenon: *wiikwegamaa* – which she translates as 'to be a bay':

> 'To be a bay' holds the wonder that, for this moment, the living water has decided to shelter itself between these shores, conversing with cedar roots and a flock of baby mergansers. Because it could do otherwise – become a stream or an ocean or a waterfall, and there are verbs for that, too…this is the language that lets us speak of what wells up around us.[4]

Kimmerer's point is part of a wide-ranging conversation on how words and stories can compel the separation of being and landscape. Philosopher David Abram writes of the loss of more-than-human connection and a degraded ability to listen to the 'living land'. Human language, he says, has 'swung in on itself, turning its back on the beings around us'.[5] Translator David Hinton, among others, contrasts the anglophone tradition with Chinese pictographic representation, pointing to the absence of the human subject in Chinese landscape painting and poetry. In the latter traditions, Hinton writes, the human hand or voice is continuous with its landscape, part of the 'single tissue' of the cosmos, an element of the 'material world that is able to touch and taste and smell itself'.[6]

Kimmerer, Abram and Hinton all notice how anglophone stories activate or engage a relationship with the landscape in which the human stands apart. They suggest an alternative story in which the human is less lonely, in live company, and in which people are also elements of the material world. I wonder what it would be like to feel this: to feel yourself a landscape, through your life. To be a personal domain, and a part of a larger environment or ecosystem: to be the bay, or the living land, or the tissue of the cosmos, which – obviously – you already are. You can feel a glass of icy water, running down your throat, a tributary to your blood supply. On cold mornings, you can see your breath become clouds, then atmosphere.

Novelist Ursula Le Guin explores what these variant stories mean for design in her essay 'The Carrier Bag Theory of Fiction', first published in 1986, but recently reissued and now more widely read and cited than it was when it first came out.[7] The essay is about storytelling, and Le Guin's argument turns on speculations about the history of design. Her contention is that the vessel (bag, pocket, basket) pre-dated the weapon (axe, knife, arrowhead) as the very first made object. From this point of origin, a whole history and philosophy of human life flows. The weapon brings about a story of heroism of hunting, conquering, extracting, taking. The bag or basket, made of 'a bit of rolled bark or leaf, or a net woven of your own hair', is made for gathering, tending, medicine or a musical instrument.

Le Guin is interested in the relationship between object and story: she looks at how they bring one another into being. The sudden, belated popularity of her essay may be related to the pressure and urgency of this connection now. Centuries of denying the environmental consequences of what we have made (or simply hoping they will go away) have only permitted those consequences to bank up. The young designer working now could be forgiven for feeling overwhelmed by the extractive histories or potential destinies of anything she could imagine. Before an invention even becomes imaginable, it must be interrogated through the many pasts and futures that could haunt it. How would we mine or fabricate its materials; where do they come from; who has rights to them; do they replenish themselves or degrade? What would happen if this object was dumped near flammable materials, or stolen by hackers, or swallowed by a migrating whale, or refurbished 700 years from now, or mistaken by an endangered bird for one of her own eggs? What would any of these emergent relationships say about you, the designer? What does your object make you?

These difficult and annoying questions are good questions. A designer who puts them to her work is thinking through just how it could be landscape. If every object seems endlessly changeable – almost too alive – this isn't necessarily a problem, but the conditions of a widened but quietly everyday awareness of precisely how all design is inherently metamorphic. The flip-flop you lost on the beach will become a turtle noose. That empty yoghurt pot could be used for growing seedlings. There is around us now a dreamy, impressionistic awareness that things are on the move through deep time and global space and this expands the range of vision. It sets human design, in its many expressions, in an alternative history of life, one that stands at variance to extractive modernity – a history in which landscape has always been a being, and all beings are landscape. including the human.

1. 'Ötzi', a glacier mummy from the Copper Age, discovered in the Ötztal Alps in 1991.
2. See Carolyn Merchant's feminist ecocritical reading of Baconianism in *The Death of Nature* (New York: Harper & Row, 1980); Peter Pesic, 'Nature on the rack: Leibniz' attitude to judicial torture and the "Torture of Nature"', *Studia Leibnitiana* 29/2 (1997), 189–97; Martin Lee Mueller's account of the long-term divisions that issued from the Cartesian split in *Being Salmon, Being Human* (White River Junction, Vermont: Chelsea Green, 2017).
3. See Anna Winterbottom, 'An experimental community: the East India Company in London, 1600-1800', *The British Journal for the History of Science* 52/2 (June 2019), 323–43.
4. Robin Wall Kimmerer, *Braiding Sweetgrass* (London: Penguin, 2020), 55.
5. David Abram, *Becoming Animal* (New York: Pantheon, 2010), 174 and passim.
6. David Hinton, *Awakened Cosmos: The Mind of Classical Chinese Poetry* (Boulder, Colorado: Shambhala, 2019), x–xi and passim.
7. Ursula Le Guin, *The Carrier Bag Theory of Fiction*, introduction. Donna Haraway (Chichester: Cosmogenesis, 2024; first published 1986).

'Noticing is my way of opposing': a conversation with Anna Tsing

Anna Tsing and Justin McGuirk

JM   Anna, your work in anthropology has been highly influential for an emerging generation of designers. And the more-than-human turn in anthropology is slowly beginning to take root in design. Indeed, you've started collaborating with designers as part of the Feral Atlas group, so today I'd like to talk about the intersection between your work and design. I'd like to begin by talking about some of your methods and terminology, which are now bleeding into design discourse. In your 2015 book *The Mushroom at the End of the World*, you elaborate a practice that you call the 'arts of noticing'. Noticing seems particularly relevant to contemporary design practice with an ecological focus – perhaps we can start there.

AT   Noticing is my way of opposing a particular modernist practice of looking towards an imagined future. Certain things get coded as possible futures and then we develop blinders so that all we can see is our trajectory towards one kind of imagined future, which isn't actually the future but is a stereotyped dream future. And so we stopped seeing. Noticing is trying to take those blinders off to look at the world around us, with special attention to the more-than-human world, by which I mean the human plus non-human world. There we start to recognise that soils are alive and, if you ship them around the world, you will spread all the living things in them, much to the detriment of the places you ship them to. And if you kill them off with fungicides and other things, they probably won't work so well for growing plants. These are little things that I think are coming back into people's observations.

Over the last few years, it's been really interesting to me to see the revival of natural history, where you can open the newspaper and find an article about a specific kind of sea worm and its reproductive habits, which was not the case before. I feel very positive about that as an attempt to open popular culture to what I'm calling noticing, or to the existence of a world around us. Despite all our attempts to squash biodiversity and landscape diversity, there are still refugia – places where all sorts of organisms still live. And I think it's important that we notice them, and maybe keep our hands off them if we want to have the kind of biodiverse earth that we take too much for granted.

JM   Noticing involves a kind of zeroing in on the particularities of a place. In your new book, *Field Guide to the Patchy Anthropocene*, you call these places 'patches' and you focus on the feral effects taking place within them, which are almost always the result of imperial or industrial infrastructure. That word 'feral' has been taken up by a number of designers. Can you speak a little bit about ferality and its relevance to design?

AT   Feral has a lot of different meanings but the core meaning in English, as I understand it, describes a domestic animal that escapes the farm and lives in the forest by itself. A pig that runs away and is perfectly capable of supporting itself in the forest? That's a feral pig. So my group stretched that meaning to look at things that come out of human plans and histories, but that escape human command and control. Just like that pig that runs away from the farm, we could look at the effects of human infrastructures and describe them as feral effects. That is, infrastructure changes its environment, and organisms change to negotiate this new world of which this infrastructure is a part.

One of the examples that I find most compelling is the water hyacinth, a water plant that was introduced to botanical gardens around the world, but escaped those gardens. This wouldn't have mattered, except that engineers were building all of these perfect places for water hyacinths to proliferate, places where the water is slow or still, like reservoirs or canals. In its original homeland in the Amazon, water hyacinth existed in fast-water streams and so it was never a problem, but if you put it in these slow-water places it starts cloning like crazy. And before you know it, it's filled the entire surface and sucked out all the oxygen. But it couldn't do it without the reservoir. So that's an example of a feral effect of infrastructure, and that's how I've been using the term.

I think it would be great if the design community was willing to use it. Because of course designers are very involved in building all kinds of things. So if we could think more about the effects of what we're building, effects that are not part of the intention or the design, that might help.

JM   The implication is that designers – masterplanners, in particular, but probably designers of all stripes – need to get better at anticipating the effects of their plans. And only by studying feral effects can they become anticipatory designers.

AT   I truly believe that. I would very much like it if designers would think about the feral effects of their projects.

JM   You've been collaborating with designers on recent projects. How do you view that relationship?

AT   Perhaps you know that Feifei Zhou and I are developing an idea for an exhibition. It's currently called *Fungi: Anarchist Designers*. It's a show with a bit of an attitude. Collaborating with designers and thinking about design

Anna Tsing in a forest near Santa Cruz, California

seems great to me. But we're also slightly worried about the way fungal mycelium has been incorporated into the design world as yet another material, just as if it were plastic or concrete. In that sense, it's become a kind of dead object, even as people make things out of it. I hadn't thought about where design begins and ends, and so this has been a concrete opportunity to think about design as a field and what kinds of dialogue I might want to have. Our show attempts to bring fungi back to life, in part by showing their ability to destroy design as we know it, to attack some of the materials that we're most dedicated to building with, especially when industrial capitalism spreads them around the world causing extinctions and all sorts of terrible things. So it's anarchism, in the sense both of attacking familiar institutions and of self-organisation and building communal worlds on their own terms, rather than on our terms.

JM   You sound sceptical about using these living things as material.

AT   No, I think there's promise to it, but I think one of the scary things about our times is the continued naturalisation of a kind of business-as-usual in which an industrial civilisation that has wreaked havoc on the natural world is just allowed to continue doing exactly what it has been doing, but each time substituting a new product that is supposed to be the miracle product.

     To get back to more-than-human worlds, let me compare that to how crops in industrial agriculture are treated, which is with real dedication to monoculture, which has to do with the need for standardisation, the control of big companies and the use of particular kinds of machines. Monoculture fields are highly susceptible to fungal attack. We know perfectly well that there are polycultural alternatives that wouldn't be nearly as vulnerable. But what we see the business world doing is substituting a new variant that's not so vulnerable to that one attack, but which of course opens it up to future attacks. So that's a comparison relevant to what I worry about in using mycelial blocks as a design element. It could be great, but as long as it supports a business-as-usual understanding of what our role in the world is, it just opens itself to future problems, a lot of which are from the misconception that when we build things to make our human lives more comfortable it has no impact on anything except us. But in fact, that's where the more-than-human approach comes in, and that's at the heart of the kind of dialogue that I would like to be having with designers.

JM   I'm interested in your analysis of monocultures or plantations as forms. In *Field Guide*, you and your co-authors dwell on the pernicious effects of these imperial and industrial forms. In fact, you explore the feral effects of modernist forms more generally, often concrete infrastructures like dams and sea walls. I wonder to what degree the problem is the form itself, or the way these forms are replicated around the world in standardised ways that don't respond to their places.

AT   What's been exciting to me over the last few years is thinking about form, in its most material meaning, as the physical manifestation of whatever it is we're talking about. A 'form' gets used to mean a style, something rather abstract. But the physical aspect of form proves to be really useful to think with. Let's go to infrastructure for a moment. The common-sense use of the term 'infrastructure' today is often 'a way to make human life better'. What's a road? Well, it's a way to get to the store more easily. What's a wall? Well, it's a way to keep the cold out. So we think of infrastructure in terms of meeting our human social needs. But if we start thinking about the physical manifestation of the form, then we can see all these other effects that occur every time we build a road or a wall. I think the problem with these imperial and industrial infrastructures is that they've been devoted to creating a world for certain kinds of powers and influences, without regard to what they're giving up.

In my current research, I'm looking at a place where swamps are being converted to dry land. If you want to have a plantation or a city, it's convenient to drain the land. What they're not thinking about is the kind of havoc that creates for all the other creatures, as well as the Indigenous people who were using the swamp *as the swamp*. And now that we know how important swamps are to the resilience of the land during climate change, it has made it possible for us to reach out to those other long-term ways that people and swamps have interacted with each other.

So it's an opportunity, an opening, to think about how we've ignored the physical manifestation of infrastructures – that is, that feature of their form as it affects the world. So, back to what you asked about uniformity versus diversity, it's not just that we spread these forms around the world,

The mushroom *Laccaria amethystina* and a swamp,
both photographed by Anna Tsing

it's that we are disregarding local environments: 'we' meaning imperial interests. And if you look at the maps of wetland loss around the world, you can see that wherever developers have gone since the European imperial age, the first thing they want to do is drain swamps. It's only very recently that elites have started thinking, 'Wait a minute, what does it mean that we just think that all local environments can get wiped out and be replaced by a particular standard environment that was thought to push forward particular kinds of interest without regard to what was being destroyed in the process?'.

JM   You suggested in an email to me that the commons and commoning are becoming relevant to your thinking again. It would be interesting to discuss how they can help foment more-than-human relations.

33

AT   I can think of many reasons why the commons are a good idea. And a number of scholars and activists are trying to create a more open notion of what could count as the commons. Even in *The Mushroom at the End of the World* I was already trying to figure out what could enter this more open commons, with a notion that I was calling 'latent commons' – commons that aren't codified as such, but have that potential as we find non-human allies in our struggles to have a liveable world. There are organisms that we want to live with, and fungi are a great example. Again, since the 1990s fungicides have been used as preventative treatment in agricultural business, so fungicide use has rocketed. This has meant removing beneficial fungi that are absolutely necessary for the soil to be good for plants at all, but also coming up with fungicide-resistant strains of fungi that will attack humans too. So we are getting rid of our fungal allies through this excessive use of fungicides. To reopen an approach towards the commons would be to allow ourselves to make friends with fungi.

JM   In a way, more-than-human thinking has to have the commons at its heart.

AT   That's right. At least, it involves living together with creatures that are different than you and imagining kinds of relationships. I mean, when I was writing *The Mushroom at the End of the World*, I had the advantage of a mutualist relationship between a mushroom and trees. But there's a variety of kinds of relations through which we can imagine our common lives. In the swamp work I'm doing, I'm thinking about commensalism, which is a relationship in which there's eating together but, unlike mutualism, one doesn't feed the other. One may not benefit when the other does. But it seems to me that the more we open the notion of the commons to multiple kinds of human and non-human relationships, the better chance we have of holding on to sites of liveability, which are very much threatened by the business-as-usual forms of ecocide.

JM   I'm interested in this because there's a form of the commons that is quite passive, which is about resources and their protection. And then there's *commoning*, which is a form of responsibility and endless negotiation, and which involves people being very active in their relationship with a place. Do you have a view on that more active role for us in those more-than-human relations?

AT   Absolutely. I don't think we can do without it. I mean, back to the fungicide example, in a parallel case, over the last 30 or 40 years the use of antibiotics has been curtailed somewhat, for exactly the same reasons as the fungicide that I was talking about – the development of antibiotic-resistant bacteria, which is going to kill us all. An example of that more active relationship is the idea that we can live with a lot of bacteria and that we don't have to be purifying every surface. I am delighted every time I hear that there's some new policy or standard through which we can reduce our reliance on antibiotics. Especially in livestock-rearing and other places where it creates a vast atmosphere of opportunities for bacteria to develop the ability to withstand all treatments. So this is just one tiny place where we need some movement towards living together – with bacteria.

The swamp work would be another example where negotiations are necessary about how people could live with the swamp. In the place where I'm working, the former dwellings were often on stilts but, because of standards of civilisation and also property law, people feel they have to fill in the swamp and drain it and put a concrete slab on top of it in order to count as a proper dwelling. So renegotiating other ways that you could live with the swamp seems to me to be in order. And that's a form of commoning. With potential commons, we have to keep reimagining what's possible.

JM   There's a term that you introduce at the end of the mushroom book that I found very useful: 'autumn thinking'. It's connected with the art of noticing, because the metaphor you elaborate is that, in autumn, we train our gaze on the forest floor looking for mushrooms, which can be difficult to spot. The implication is that we live in a time when things aren't so abundant and we have to be more resourceful.

AT   Yes, I think for a lot of the twentieth century, which is still very much with us, the idea that growth solves all problems cut across the work of economists, developers, designers and many other fields. And the kinds of problems growth was expected to solve included racial conflict, scarcities and all sorts of other things, at the same time transforming the world into platforms for corporate interests. That's not working out very well, shall we say. I feel quite inspired by the movements of degrowth, on the one hand, and unbuilding on the other. And I feel excited that some designers will find great opportunities in thinking with questions about how to work in a world that's not about the stable truisms of the twentieth century. This could be a great time for design.

But, as I said earlier, this must be coupled with a real engagement with the material world. If design gets abstracted from the world, without paying attention to the world, then it's going to be part of the problem. But a design in which engagement with the world is part of what designers do? Then it's a really exciting place to think about both the problems and the possibilities of what's ahead.

Hélio Melo was an artist and rubber tapper who navigated difficult paths through the Brazilian Amazon to extract latex from rubber trees. Melo documented this way of life in his paintings. Here, the tree branches become a map charting the tapper's route. The tree-map symbolises the relationship between human and forest – one that was being replaced by more destructive industries, such as cattle farming and mining.

Hélio Melo, *Mapa da Estrada (Seringa)* [Map of the Road (Rubber tree)], 1998

Solange Pessoa's figures cannot be clearly read as human, animal or vegetable. They may be all three, or captured mid-metamorphosis. The figures seem to reject boundaries between one form of life and another, evoking a fluid life force. Many of Pessoa's works recall the animist beliefs of Brazil's Indigenous peoples, in which all forms of life have spirit or agency.

Solange Pessoa, *Untitled*, from the *Sonhíferas* (Dreamers) series, 2020–21

APRIL

01 ... The mating season has started for adders; the males compete in a dance to impress females.
02 ... The first chiffchaffs have returned and begin to sing their name.
03 ... The first young of the wild boar are born.
04 ... The first willow warbler song can be heard.
05 ... Tadpoles abound in ponds and pools.
06 ... Sparrowhawks and kestrels are nesting.
07 ... The first nightingales return.
08 ... Most buzzards have laid their first egg.
09 ... The distinctive orange-tip butterflies are flying.
10 ... Grass snakes are mating.
11 ... Male cuckoos begin to arrive from Sub-Saharan Africa and start calling their name.
12 ... Beavers are having their first young.
13 ... Ash trees are flowering.
14 ... Yellow wagtails have arrived from their winter retreats.
15 ... Hedgehogs are emerging from hibernation.
16 ... The small tortoiseshell butterfly and comma butterfly are at the peak of their flight period.
17 ... Young mallards are hatching and can be seen swimming.
18 ... Crab apples are flowering.
19 ... Grey squirrels prepare their dreys (tree nests).
20 ... Yellow archangel in flower.
21 ... Pied flycatchers and grasshopper warblers have returned from migration.
22 ... Pedunculate or English oak leaves unfolding.
23 ... Hawthorn hedgerows begin to blossom.
24 ... The wood warbler has arrived to spend the summer.
25 ... Great and blue tits are now sitting on eggs.
26 ... Rare migrating turtle doves that have survived being hunted while crossing Malta arrive in UK.
27 ... The first flowers of the horse chestnut tree are appearing.
28 ... The reed warbler is in the country.
29 ... The first swifts have arrived and will stay for one hundred days.
30 ... The male wren is busy making several nests, the female chooses one of them.

This calendar lists specific events taking place in the natural world throughout the year. Animals and plants are oblivious to our calendar days and months, but respond to shifts in temperature, light and magnetic currents that we cannot sense. Coates' work is a reminder that humans once used close observation of other species to track the movements of seasons.

MAY

01 ... Female cuckoos are arriving.

02 ... The first nightjars arrive, churring and wing clapping at dusk.

03 ... Wild bluebells are in full flower in the woods.

04 ... Young tawny owls may be calling now, before they have broken out of their egg.

05 ... The first young grebes have hatched and are carried on the backs of their parents.

06 ... Spotted flycatchers are arriving from Africa.

07 ... The rare golden oriole's fluting song might be heard.

08 ... Oaks are in flower, producing a lot of pollen.

09 ... Holly blue butterflies are on the wing.

10 ... The last of the summer migrants have arrived: swifts are screaming across the sky.

11 ... Oxeye daisy in flower.

12 ... Butterflies abound: speckled wood, wall brown, green-veined white, dingy skipper on the wing.

13 ... Meadow froghoppers are appearing from their foam 'cuckoo spit' nests on plant stems.

14 ... Young moles are being born.

15 ... Young eels start ascending rivers from the sea.

16 ... Bogbean and yellow iris in flower along the banks of ponds.

17 ... The air is full of blackbird song.

18 ... Ash are coming into leaf, one of the last trees of the spring.

19 ... Swallowtail butterflies are on the wing.

20 ... The first red deer calves of the year are being born.

21 ... Young great tits are leaving their nests.

22 ... Most swifts have laid an egg under loose roof tiles.

23 ... Mistle thrushes cease singing, their work done.

24 ... Fox cubs are emerging from their earths and playing above the ground.

25 ... Common spotted orchid, common mallow, yellow tattle are in flower.

26 ... Brightly coloured garden tiger moths are on the wing.

27 ... Hummingbird hawk-moths are on the wing, looking for nectar.

28 ... The first caddisflies are emerging from water.

29 ... Robins have their second brood; the young of the first brood have left their nest.

30 ... Meadows are full of buttercups.

31 ... Poisonous hound's tongue is in flower.

Marcus Coates, *Nature Calendar*, 2022

These baskets were woven by members of the Ye'kuana people of the Venezuelan Amazon. Weaving baskets is central to Ye'kuana identity. It is a ritual process that begins with songs, asking the rainforest's permission to take the necessary materials for weaving. The Ye'kuana view baskets as sacred objects, essentially an extension of the natural world. They are often decorated with the animals of the forest. These types, the small Jojo and the larger Wüwa, are only woven by women.

Wüwa basket with frogs by Felicia, 2020–23
Opposite: *Wüwa* baskets by Dawa and Marieta, 2020–23
Overleaf: *Wüwa* and *Jojo* baskets by Dawa and Rosalinda, 2020–23

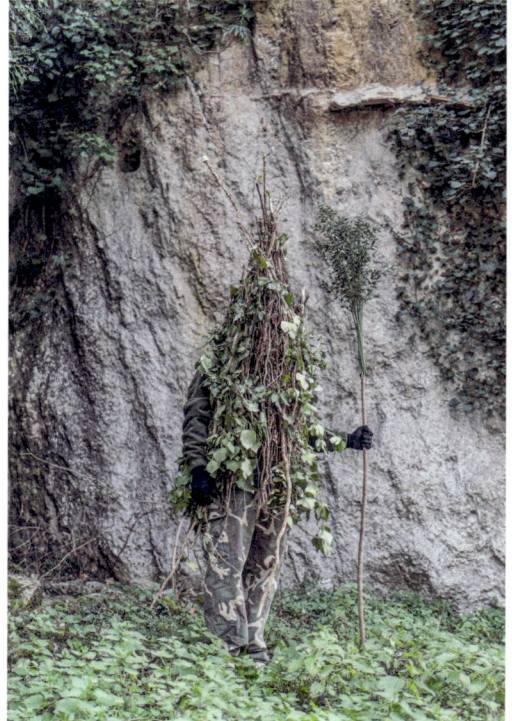

Every year during carnival, participants clad in leaves collected from local woodland parade into the town of Satriano di Lucania in southern Italy. Called rumiti – from the Italian for 'hermit' – these figures have emerged from both Christian traditions and pagan folklore. The festival was revived by younger generations of the region in 2012 to celebrate the ways in which we continue to be entangled with the landscapes around us.

Federico Borella, Michela Balboni, *Rumita*, 2024

Jonathan Baldock, who comes from a family of hop-gatherers and gardeners, researches traditions in which communities celebrate their relationship with the land. This series of masks is inspired by corn dollies like those shown overleaf, which were made throughout Europe for hundreds of years. Originally made from corn and worn for a performance, they were later cast into bronze, transforming an ephemeral, seasonal object into a permanent record of the skill of its maker.

48

Jonathan Baldock, *Corn Dolly II–VI*, 2013–23

Corn dollies were traditionally made from the stalks of the last sheaf of grain to be harvested each year. Plaited into staffs, wreaths or even human forms, they were kept to preserve life through the fallow months until the following spring. The practice was widespread in Europe but died out in the mid-twentieth century. James Richardson made his traditional dolly in 1935 at the age of 93, while Fred Mizen's shepherd's crook design was exhibited at the Festival of Britain in 1951, a public celebration of British design and craft.

Fred Mizen, *Strawcraft shepherd's crook*, 1951
Opposite: James Richardson, *Corn dolly*, 1935

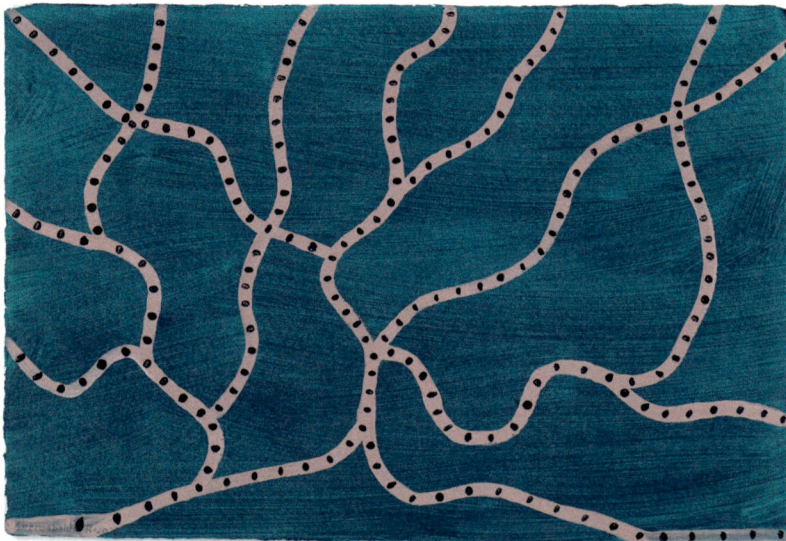

Sheraonawe Hakihiiwe is part of the Yanomami Indigenous community who live in the Venezuelan and Brazilian Amazon. His paintings record details that he observes around him in the forest, from patterns used by his mother to decorate his body as a child and the surface of baskets she wove, to traces left by animals and the forms of plants and trees. Together, they form an archive of Yanomami knowledge that reflects the abundance of life in the forest.

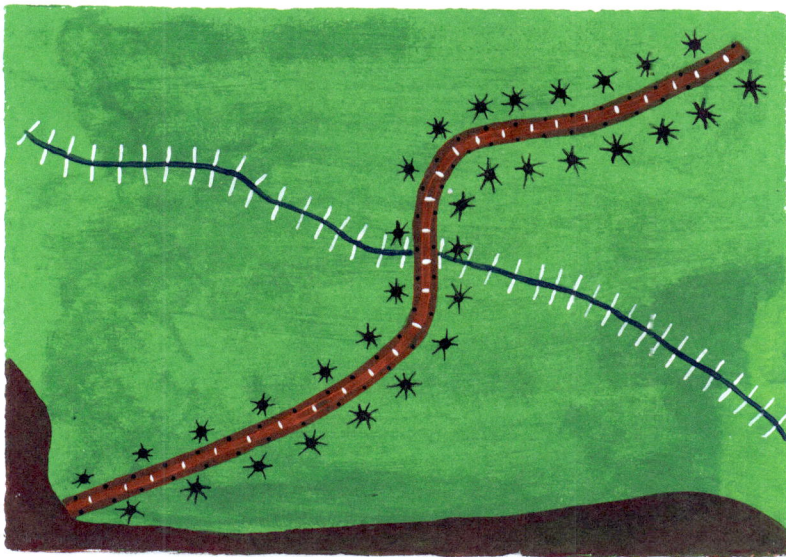

Clockwise from top: Sheroanawe Hakahiiwe, *Masiko kekipi* [Palms of spirits that fan the world], *Hii yao yao hoko sike riye* [Ocelot stick and green palm], *Mapari peno mayo* [Another path of termites], *Pei yono uhutipi* [Spirit of the path], 2023

This video combines oral histories with historical and contemporary photographs, cartography and gaming software to map the changes in the Omaheke region of Namibia.
Humans, plants and landscapes all become witnesses to the long-term effects of German colonisation. The work supports demands for ancestral lands to be returned to the
people of the region and reparations paid. It was initiated by the collectives Forensic
Architecture and Forensis, in partnership with The Ovaherero/Ovambanderu Genocide
Foundation (OGF).

Forensic Architecture, Forensis, video still from *The Environmental Continuum of Genocide in Namibia*, 2025

What can forests teach us about the cosmos and our place within it? Ursula Biemann brings together Indigenous ritual practice and Western scientific research to answer this question. The film's voiceover, provided by Biemann, explores ways of expressing the intersections of knowledge between Indigenous medics and molecular biologists. *Forest Mind* stems from the artist's long-term research work with the Inga people of the Colombian Amazon and brings the forest into the exhibition through a sample of Amazonian DNA which is embedded in the installation.

Ursula Biemann, video stills from *Forest Mind*, 2021

César Rodriguez-Garavito, Elena Landinez and the More-Than-Human
Life (MOTH) collective, *The More-Than-Human Rights Mural*, 2025

More-than-human rights are as much a legal proposition as they are a story about our relationship with the more-than-human world. For their fellowship, the MOTH collective, led by César Rodriguez-Garavito, created *The More-Than-Human Rights Mural*. The mural frames the hundreds of initiatives recognizing the rights of nature worldwide as efforts to tell a story where human and non-human animals, plants, fungi, rivers, forests, oceans and other ecosystems are all animate and entangled in the planetary web of life.

The work focuses on rivers as living beings and legal subjects. The most successful legal actions of this sort have sought to protect rivers by granting them rights to survive and thrive. Moreover, the fractal shape of watersheds visually represents the commonality and interconnectedness of different forms of life. The mural centres around the fractal drawing of a watershed, where the main river and its tributaries are represented as living beings containing other living beings. The artist Elena Landinez, who creates the imagery for the MOTH Program, imagined these beings as composites of various life forms.

To invite viewers to actively engage with MOTH rights stories through their own experiences, thoughts and emotions, the mural asks two questions: 'Water is speaking. What is it saying?' and 'Who are your rivers?' *The More-Than-Human Rights Mural* tells a dynamic story. It acknowledges both the harms suffered by living rivers – through pollution, damming, and other threats – and the potential for their revival. To capture this dynamism, Landinez's design offers visitors two distinct versions of the mural. When viewed through red-lens glasses, a panoply of new shapes and texts emerges, offering a glimpse into the richness of ideas and actions from around the world that shape the MOTH rights field. The texts include excerpts from constitutional provisions, court rulings and declarations enshrining the rights of rivers and rights of nature more broadly.

More than Human Fellow

César Rodríguez-Garavito, Elena Landinez, *The More-Than-Human Rights Mural*, 2025

IS A RIVER ALIVE?

WHAT ARE THEY SAYING?

WHO ARE YOUR RIVERS?

MOTH RIGHTS (MORE-THAN-HUMAN)

César Rodríguez-Garavito, Elena Landinez, *The More-Than-Human Rights Mural*, 2025

Paulo Tavares, *Earthly Memorials: São Paulo Terra Indígena (São Paulo Indigenous Land)*, 2025

Earthly Memorials is a long-term exploration of landscapes that challenge ideas of nature in heritage and preservation. For the fellowship Paulo Tavares developed *Earthly Memorials: São Paulo Terra Indígena*. In collaboration with Guarani teachers, leaders, activists and architecture students, the project focused on building a spatial advocacy platform to support the recognition and protection of forest heritage in the Jaraguá Guarani Indigenous Land in the city of São Paulo. Surrounded by the city's voracious urban sprawl, the Jaraguá Peak – a symbolic geological-geographic feature – is home to the only remnant of Atlantic Forest in São Paulo, the most devastated Brazilian biome since European colonialism.

As well as being an ecological area of fundamental importance for the climate regulation of São Paulo, a city where green spaces are notoriously scarce, the Jaraguá is a territory of immense heritage value for the Guarani nation. With the continuous expansion of São Paulo, the Guarani's sacred forests are constantly under threat of development. The fellowship supported the production of a multimedia heritage dossier on the Jaraguá Guarani Land. Combining data analysis, oral history, audiovisual documentation and archival material, the dossier is generating an advocacy tool in support of more-than-human rights and the ongoing struggle of the Guarani for reparation and land rights recognition.

In addition to the audio-visual installation, the heritage dossier includes a map of the Jaraguá produced with the community. The dossier, which will be published in Guarani and Portuguese, will be shared with the Guarani *tekohas* in a series of collective workshops on land, city and heritage rights. The design research thus becomes an advocacy tool with local impact.

Spanning design, pedagogy, publishing and rights advocacy, the project has been developed in collaboration with the Jaraguá Guarani Land (with the researchers Anthony Karaí Poty and Thiago Henrique Karai Djekupe, and the filmmaker Richard Werã), the Chão collective and the Spatial Practices Platform of Escola da Cidade in São Paulo.

More than Human Fellow

Map of the Jaraguá Guarani Indigenous Land being used by the Guarani in a land demarcation ceremony

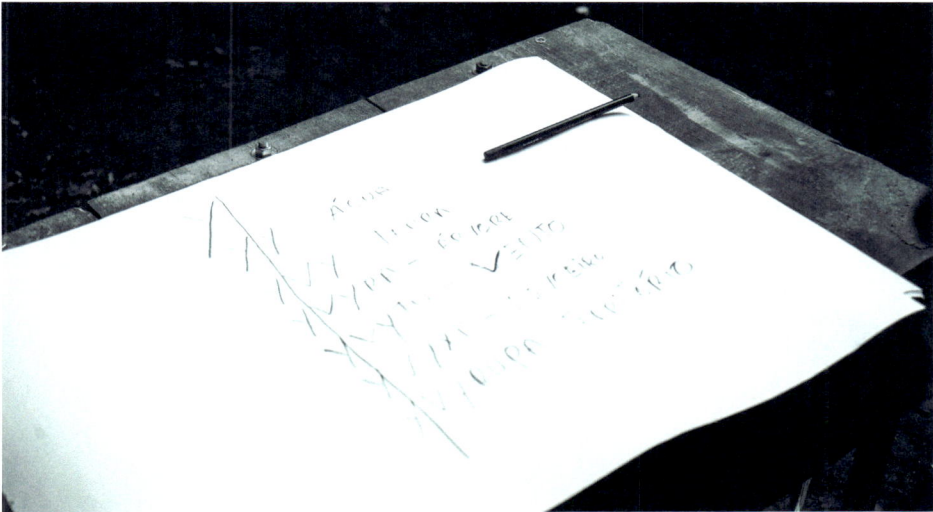

Paulo Tavares, video stills from *Earthly Memorials: São Paulo Terra Indígena*, 2025

II

Making with the World

Johanna Seelemann, *Oase* (Oasis) *W1*, 2023

Everything we make is an expression of our relationship with our planet and its inhabitants, whether we are aware of it or not. In the face of ongoing climate change, designers, architects and artists working today have a greater responsibility than ever to consider and support wild species, even whole ecosystems, with their work. If we look beyond the industrialised West for reminders of human behaviours that think beyond human needs, examples of care and cohabitation are abundant, especially for our closest companion species. But how to go about answering this planetary-scale challenge?

The projects discussed in this chapter attempt to create support structures, encourage biodiversity and have regenerative effects. They are taking place in areas as diverse as architectural facades, coastal regions, multispecies habitats and objects for human use. Architect Andrés Jaque proposes an architecture that does not separate human bodies from the world but, rather, encourages a continuous exchange between living things. Designer James Peplow Powell argues in favour of observing and designing for the many species that we have always lived alongside, but from whom we have become increasingly distant. Scholar and curator Jia Yi Gu examines the shift in thinking required by making with microscopic living systems such as bacteria and mycelium.

It is in the breadth and variety of the projects included here that we can perhaps locate a definition for more-than-human design: this way of thinking must pay attention to the needs of many different species and systems at a local, even microscopic level. And it is by embracing multiple approaches, places and scales that more-than-human design becomes an expression of the complexity of the world.

Rebecca Lewin

The more-than-human city: designing for coexistence

James Peplow Powell

If you live in a city in the Global North, the chances are your immediate environment is dominated by designs that neglect, exclude or exploit the non-human world. It has not always been so. Consider the room you are in now, the building, and the street outside. Now start to rewind: 50 years, a hundred years, two hundred. What changes? Modern appliances and products disappear, as do plastics. Building materials transform into stone, timber, straw and other agricultural by-products: locally sourced, rougher-edged, looser-fitting. Through the resulting gaps, a bird or a bat moves into the eaves or a wall cavity, while inside the house the family expands to include multiple generations and then multiple species: cattle, horses, goats and other domesticated animals.

Outside, the street, city and landscape beyond are shaped, too, by unfamiliar cultural and ecological practices. In Ottoman Istanbul, food and water is laid out in the street for urban animals, in dishes set into paving slabs, or thrown up into the sky to circling hawks.[1] In rural Honshu, Japan, water comes not from a tap but a *kabata*: a covered basin, built into a stream, complete with resident carp that keep the water clean. Across Europe and Asia, the landscape is marked by strange towers: dovecotes, which house doves and pigeons for the purposes of messaging, leather-tanning and agricultural fertility, or *dakhma* – towers of silence – in which humans are laid after death to be eaten by vultures, in a final and profound act of ecological generosity.

Today, these structures – and the more-than-human relationships they hosted – lie in ruins, replaced by the ubiquitous products of industrial design. A motorised vehicle, a phone, a bathroom tap: all have been designed to replace a previous interdependence with animals and ecosystems, and all obscure the myriad ways they still impact on and extract from other species on their journey from raw material to finished product along unseen global supply chains. Instead, our relations to other species are carefully curated: isolated to parks, gardens and natural reserves, designed for the therapeutic needs of human urban residents, or as a last resort for species flatlining towards extinction. But what about the diversity of species we used to live alongside?

Modern life makes characteristic separations – between nature and culture, city and wilderness, human and non-human.[2] These ways of seeing the world mean the city is rarely considered a more-than-human habitat, preventing the needs of other forms of life from influencing the design of the urban spaces and objects that surround us. Take, for instance, the celebrated and ubiquitous 'glass box' of modern architecture, from the Bauhaus to the contemporary office block. We might celebrate the technical achievements of such buildings, yet the glass which enables such structures is so transparent and reflective that it is impossible for many species to see. Combined with artificial lighting, our cities have become confounding to the senses of birds and insects, leading to billions of their deaths every year.[3]

The problems posed by glass are easily preventable with a little consideration of the way that birds see the world. The designer Kate Orff of SCAPE, for instance, has compiled a set of guidelines for bird-safe buildings, which can be used both for the design of new structures and the rehabilitation of existing ones.[4] The differences between human and bird vision can even be used to advantage: by using films, diachronic coatings and applied patterns in the UV spectrum, glass can be made opaque to many birds, even while remaining transparent to humans. It's an important place to start to undo the damage, which we can all apply to the windows of our dwellings, although it still represents little more than a sticking plaster.

Rather than just mitigating harm, how might contemporary design actively support more generous and mutually supportive forms of coexistence once again? It's a question explored by the designer Johanna Seelemann. With a focus on everyday urban products, she explores how they might be redesigned to benefit both humans and multiple other species.[5] Her Habitat Façade is an architectural element that forms the external walls of buildings while providing nesting spaces for insects as well as birds. Animals have made homes in the gaps and eaves of buildings for thousands of years, and some – such as swifts – now nest nowhere else, but these animals have been negatively impacted by modern buildings and construction products that seal up these gaps and imperfections. In

72

turn, products such as 'swift bricks' are increasingly being integrated into buildings to provide these spaces once more.[6] With her Habitat Façade, alongside elements that provide for urban foraging – Enzo Mari's Milanese Panettone concrete bollards are reinterpreted as urban seed bombs, and low-fired terracotta vases redeploy an ancient irrigation system to provide water to urban trees – Seelemann suggests how such ecological offerings could more profoundly shape the formal and material languages of the city.

Finnish architects Maiju Suomi and Elina Koivisto similarly explore how cities might provide for both humans and other species, such as birds and insects. Their Alusta Pavilion is also an extension of an increasingly common design product for urban animals: the 'insect hotel'. These structures, made from porous materials such as ceramic pots, bricks, logs and reeds, provide a range of intimate nesting spaces for insects. At the Alusta Pavilion,

Pigeon dovecotes in Egypt, date unknown

such materials are expanded to a human-sized pavilion within a landscape of pollinator-friendly plants, utilising familiar and affordable building products in innovative ways. It's both easy and inspiring to imagine these materials proliferating across small urban sites, pavements and planters, as a supportive infrastructure for urban invertebrates.

More-than-human design, on the other hand, is never less everyday than in the work of Studio Ossidiana. Their colourful work elevates the presence of wildlife in the city through carefully crafted, sculptural landscapes, which combine a precise aesthetic sensibility with a great generosity towards the more-than-human world. Their ornamental bird perches, a recurring motif in their work, recall those of intricate Victorian birdcages, but here they stand freely in the landscape. The implication is clear: the private enclosure of wildlife is handed over to the common reintegrating the bird into a wider habitat and resituating the long history of the enjoyment of, care for and spectacle of birds within public space, open to the participation of all.

Building joyful cohabitation back into our homes and cities is fundamental to more-than-human design, but, at the same time, we cannot design for species to return without also rethinking human activities that are causing their ongoing decline. How might redesigning urban cohabitation help address these wider problems? In 'Dovecote for London', I consider this challenge with the help of an animal that is already thriving in urban environments: the feral pigeon. The presence of these birds in our cities – though not universally celebrated – is a legacy of their domestication and their past utility to people. This use is recorded, too, in the ubiquity of pigeon towers – or dovecotes – which were built across Europe and Asia in pre-industrial times as infrastructure for nutrient circularity.[7] The towers housed the birds and collected their fertile guano (droppings) as a sustainable source of fertility for agriculture. Over the nineteenth and twentieth centuries, dovecotes were replaced by mining and then industrially synthesising ammonia through the Haber process, becoming a major contributor to the profound disruption of global climate and ecosystems. Meanwhile, the redundant pigeon has found a home in urban environments, becoming a management problem for urban estates and institutions, such as Transport for London, who attempt – ultimately unsuccessfully – to exclude the birds from their buildings and infrastructure. Instead, 'Dovecote for London' proposes a network of care for urban pigeons that captures their problematic guano and redistributes it in a circular network of fertility for urban farms. While modern, energy-intensive industrial technologies may seem to have irreversibly replaced many ancient interspecies partnerships, designers could yet reimagine a place for them in the future.

While urban spaces have become home for many non-human animals, some other species far exceed humans in their abilities to shape their environments for themselves and others. Indeed, the largest structures of biological origin on earth are made by tiny marine animals: corals.[8] Their reefs, collectively built over centuries from the limestone backbones of generations of corals, can stretch for many thousands of kilometres. These structures are teeming with life: despite covering less than 1% of the ocean seafloor, they provide a home for over a quarter of marine species.[9] The unique complexity of reef architecture provides for countless nurseries, safehouses and other habitats for fish and other marine animals, while reefs offer more than one billion coastal peoples food, livelihoods and essential protection from storm surges and tsunamis. Whether the value of corals should be encapsulated in economic terms is debatable, but a study in 2020 totalled their annual contributions through ecosystem services at $11 trillion,[10] dwarfing the economic output of all but two nations,[11] as well as almost matching the entire human design and construction sectors.[12]

Having supported more-than-human life on our planet for over 450 million years, coral reefs could disappear forever within the coming decades. They have already declined by more than half since the 1950s due to human activities such as extractive fishing practices, shipping and marine construction, and algal blooms caused by sewage and fertiliser run-off, and they are projected to decline a further 99% in the coming decades due to global heating. While corals can regenerate themselves after damage, these impacts are now too severe and frequent: if corals are the 'cities of the sea',[13] humans are taking a bulldozer to them faster than they can rebuild.

What if human intervention could instead catalyse the repair of this critical ecological infrastructure? This is the idea behind MARS – the Modular Artificial Reef Structure. Designed by Reef Design Lab, a Melbourne-based multidisciplinary studio led by industrial designer Alex Goad, it's a flexible modular system that can be used to restore and extend

Reef Design Lab, *Modular Artificial Reef Structure ('MARS)*, 2022

the physical infrastructure of damaged reefs. The ceramic modules, slip-cast in a 3D-printed mould, re-create the complex topology and 'cellular structure'[14] of a reef's bedrock, providing a robust substrate for the growth of young corals and secure refuge for some of the countless animals displaced by the loss of natural reefs.

MARS has been deployed on test sites including a sandy seabed in the Maldives with no existing reef, which represented the largest artificial reef of its kind. Six years since installation, the structure has been transformed by profusion of coral growth and new resident fish, creating a flourishing ecosystem from almost nothing. The success of MARS is also in its shaping of human relationships with the reef. Humans have a surprisingly long history of intervention in aquatic ecosystems: artificial reefs have been built since ancient times for sustainable fishing and aquaculture in places such as Japan and the Philippines,[15] and have been used for conservation since the 1950s. However, typical artificial reefs are megastructures of concrete blocks and steel cages: materials that, while cheap and freely available, are high in embodied carbon, corrosive to marine life, and require cumbersome ships and machinery to install. Reef Design Lab's ceramic MARS system avoids these issues, as the lightweight modules can be installed on the seafloor by local divers from small fishing boats, expanding the possible locations of intervention. In turn, this fosters a sense of stewardship and care among the local human communities who depend on reefs, as Alex Goad explains, 'because they've physically installed it themselves'.[16]

Kate Orff's Living Breakwaters project, similarly, focuses on restoring the beneficial functions of coastal reefs, while working in a more northerly context and at an infrastructural scale. The project submerged nearly 700 metres of stone and ecologically enhanced concrete units off the southern

Studio Ossidiana, *The City of Birds*, 2019–22

shore of Staten Island, New York. These 'breakwaters' are designed to re-duce the impact of climate-intensified storm surges and to reverse decades of beach erosion, while also providing habitat for oysters on reef 'ridges' and 'streets'. It has become a model for 'nature-based infrastructure': a living support system and more-than-human partnership that develops mutual resilience in the face of climatic and ecological threats.

These aquatic infrastructures are fascinating expansions of what design can do: humans have long created tools, shelters and infrastructures to extend the habitable regions of the planet for our own benefit and the benefit of a small range of companion animals, but rarely to support wild ecosystems as complex as reefs, or animals with lifeworlds as alien to ours as those of a coral or an oyster. Active intervention to support complex ecologies, or even create them from scratch, is however approached with some caution by those already working closely with the more-than-human world.[17] The act of installing a prefabricated artificial reef, for instance, is radically different from the iterative growth of natural infrastructure, which is shaped by a dizzying diversity of ecological relationships forged over centuries. How resilient might these more-than-human design collaborations prove in the long run?

Navigating these treacherous and uncharted waters requires the development of more radical forms of collaboration, not just in multi-*disciplinary* but in multi-*species* terms, and a repositioning of the human designer within an expanded assemblage of more-than-human expertise. Successful more-than-human design relies on collaboration between human and more-than-human designers, but the process of participation raises questions: with such a diversity of species in any ecosystem, whose preferences should we favour? And how do we know that our intervention is a genuine contribution to an ecology, rather than merely creating a trap, attracting certain species away from more suitable sites, like moths to a lamp?[18]

Ultimately, we don't have the luxury of time to find out: with human disruption already happening everywhere through habitat disruption and climate change, interventions are required before the true consequences can be understood. Global temperatures have already breached the UN's critical threshold of 1.5° above pre-industrial levels for over a year,[19] and are on track for more than 3° warming. This will lead to a near-total loss of coral reefs worldwide, not to mention accelerated species extinction and severe disruption to the diversity of more-than-human infrastructures that we all depend on.[20] More-than-human designers, alongside ecologists and researchers, can help some ecosystems temporarily resist these pressures, but the sobering reality remains that their efforts will be futile unless wider design cultures can be challenged and overturned.

More-than-human designs such as artificial reefs may appear to be temporary measures – reparative acts in an era of irresponsibility – but they prompt us to reconsider the obligations of all designers to the more-than-human world. Ultimately, all acts of design have ecological implications: it's up to us whether they are damaging or restorative. It's a daunting realisation, but one that invites all of us to participate in the project of recovery. Whether in the restoration of coral 'cities' or in the ongoing care for our local urban communities, how might we return to our collective challenges re-energised by the wonder and the precarity of our shared, more-than-human world?

1. Baron Wenceslas Wratislaw, 1591, in *The Adventures of Baron Wenceslas Wratislaw of Mitrowitz* (Cambridge: Cambridge University Press, 2013).

2. As extensively critiqued by those such as Bruno Latour (*We Have Never Been Modern*, trans. Catherine Porter (Cambridge, Massachusetts: Harvard University Press, 1993)) and William Cronon ('The trouble with wilderness; or, getting back to the wrong nature', in *Uncommon Ground: Rethinking the Human Place in Nature*, ed. William Cronon (New York: W.W. Norton & Co., 1995), 69–90.

3. Ar Kornreich, et al., 'Rehabilitation outcomes of bird–building collision victims in the Northeastern United States', *PLOS One* 19/8: e0306362, https://doi.org/10.1371/journal.pone.0306362 [Accessed 3 April 2025].

4. The guidelines can be downloaded from Kate Orff's website: https://www.scapestudio.com/projects/bird-safe-building-guidelines/.

5. Johanna Seelemann, *Micrographia*, https://johannaseelemann.com/Micrographia-1 [Accessed 9 January 2025].

6. For example, the swift brick by Manthorpe Building Products was developed in conjunction with the RSPB: https://www.manthorpebp.co.uk/swift-brick. Alongside those of other manufacturers, several tens of thousands of these bricks have been installed in homes in the UK.

7. See James Peplow Powell, 'Dovecote for London', in *Islands* (London: Future Observatory, 2023), https://futureobservatory.org/research/library?paper=islands-design-researchers-in-residence-2022-2023 [Accessed 3 April 2025].

8. 'What is the Great Barrier Reef?', National Ocean Service, https://oceanservice.noaa.gov/facts/gbrlargeststructure.html [Accessed 9 January 2025].

9. 'Census of Marine Life' (2010), http://www.coml.org [Accessed 3 April 2025].

10. Hanny E. Rivera, Andrea N. Chan and Victoria Luu, 'Coral reefs are critical for our food supply, tourism, and ocean health. We can protect them from climate change', *Science Policy Review*, https://sciencepolicyreview.org/2020/08/coral-reefs-are-critical-for-our-food-supply-tourism-and-ocean-health-we-can-protect-them-from-climate-change/ [Accessed 3 April 2025].

11. The US and China.

12. The global creative industries sector is estimated at $2 trillion and the global construction sector at $9.7 trillion in 2022; see https://www.oxfordeconomics.com/resource/global-construction-futures/ [Accessed 3 April 2025].

13. As described by the Natural History Museum exhibition *Coral Reefs: Secret Cities of the Sea* (2015).

14. Alex Goad's 2017 interview with Questacon – the National Science and Technology Centre, Canberra: 'Alex Goad on artificial reefs and what makes MARS so special | Enterprising Australians', https://www.youtube.com/watch?v=lCQph-n90Ro&list=PLWiPssHyl_QmEdHAiZ017xPbTarqyYKVb&index=12 [Accessed 3 April 2025].

15. Shinya Otake, 'Design and creation of fishing grounds in Japan with artificial reefs', *Modern Fisheries Engineering* (Boca Raton, Florida: CRC Press, 2020).

16. Ibid.

17. Graham Readfearn, 'As record heat risks bleaching 73% of the world's coral reefs, scientists ask "what do we do now?"', *The Guardian*, 29 July 2024, https://www.theguardian.com/environment/article/2024/jul/30/as-record-heat-risks-bleaching-73-of-the-worlds-coral-reefs-scientists-ask-what-do-we-do-now [Accessed 3 April 2025].

18. Interview with Anja Wegner (Max Planck Institute of Animal Behavior), 17 October 2024.

19. '1.5°C: what it means and why it matters', United Nations: Climate Action, https://www.un.org/en/climatechange/science/climate-issues/degrees-matter [Accessed 21 January 2025].

20. Intergovernmental Panel on Climate Change, 'Special Report on Global Warming of 1.5°C', 8 October 2018.

Trans-species architecture

Andrés Jaque

Architects think that they design the buildings that life will later occupy. The term they use for when life has moved in is 'post-occupancy'. But dividing the world into occupied and occupying entities is fundamentally naive. Bodies, buildings, environments and climates are intrinsically inseparable.[1] Design is the redesign of how they affect each other, with the redesign of one being the redesign of all. For example, the concrete that forms a building is an ecosystem in which fungi, moss and bacteria dwell. Similarly, particles that were once part of a concrete wall will find themselves suspended in the air, only to be breathed in and eaten by humans, cats and birds, becoming blood, and defecated out. The CO_2 leaving our lungs will enter the porous concrete and be mineralised by microbes and plants, becoming part of the concrete. Flesh and container are inseparable. Considering how any given material is inevitably an ecosystem, design is always a rearticulation of existing entities, many of them life-bearing. By intervening in how a multitude of entities articulate their coexistence, architecture defines new interdependencies. For instance, it makes some species more likely to survive and proliferate, and others more likely to perish or be sacrificed. I call this 'trans-species architecture'.

Trans-species architecture is not about space, nor is it about form. It is the way different sensing entities enact their physical, neuronal and metabolic entanglement – the way they constitute themselves as inseparable. Architecture is the means by which different entities co-produce each other as a bodied and environmentalised togetherness. Trans-species architecture makes the fleshy and the mineral, the technological and the biological, indistinguishable. Any given body is collective. Any given body is an assembly of diverse forms of life and non-life. Bodying is bodying collectiveness. Bodies infiltrate other bodies and are infiltrated by living and non-living entities. They become environment and climate. Climate is environments, bodies, land, minerals, earthiness, wetness, technologies becoming enacted-togetherness. Any given body is body-environmental. Trans-species architecture claims that any architecture is a more-than-human architecture, and as such it redefines cities, buildings and bodies not as self-contained but as collective and distributed. These relationships depend on a type of politics that often exceeds the spectrum of human consciousness. The medium for this politics is not the spoken word but the realm of physical and material entanglement. The philosopher Isabelle Stengers referred to these politics as 'cosmopolitics'.[2] Since its founding in 2003, my practice, the Office for Political Innovation, has focused on moving away from anthropocentrism and extractivism to explore architectures that promote more symmetrical ways for humans to relate to more-than-human life.

One could argue that modern architecture was born out of the attempt to put the more-than-human richness of the world under the control of Western men. The Lily House at Chatsworth in Derbyshire, England, is often considered a seminal reference in the development of modern architecture. This greenhouse, designed by Joseph Paxton in 1849, pioneered the development of glass architecture. Whereas it is often analysed through its lightness and transparency, the full complexity of its design can only be understood when its interspecies performance is taken into account. It was designed to secure the British Empire's control of the blossoming of the gigantic *Victoria amazonica* more than 6,000 miles from its habitat in Bolivia, where it had been extracted during Robert Schomburgk's imperial botanic expeditions.[3] Both the invention of a hidden water-heating system and of its glass envelope responded to Queen Victoria's call for architects to compete to achieve human power over the lilies' reproduction. Later, Mies van der Rohe's interior pool for lilies and papyrus in the Villa Tugendhat of 1930 followed Paxton's inventions and eco-colonial vision. Similarly, Mies's German National Pavilion in Barcelona was nothing other than a showroom to promote Germany's emerging capacity to extract and commercialise the geological richness of a small number of Latin American ecosystems at the 1929 world fair.[4] Even the creation of the United States Forest Service has been read as a way to achieve human administrative control over more-than-human life.[5] These projects show how there are robust threads in modern architecture focused on intervening in the way human life is imposed on other forms of life. In a variety of ways, these designs shared the ultimate mission of enforcing the supremacy of human power, and operated through anthropocentrism. Most recently, projects such as the Hybrid Muscle pavilion in Chiang Mai, Thailand, by Philippe Parreno in 2002 – which includes an ox labouring to provide ventilation for humans – make the design of interspecies relationships an explicit terrain for architecture, but also in a way that confirms human centrality and the subjugation of other forms of life. If these are precedents of how architecture operates in the design of interspecies coexistence, they are all part of the paradigm of anthropocentrism that trans-species architecture confronts.

The *trans* in trans-species architecture refers to the impossibility of defining any life as human-only. It is a way to confirm that life itself is in

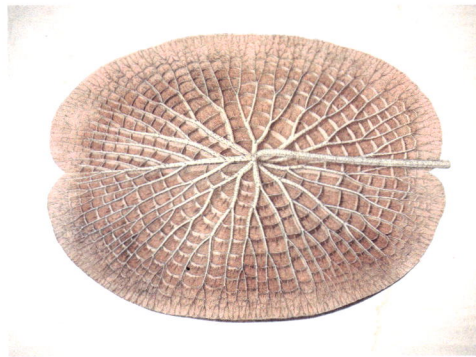

William Sharp, illustration of a *Victoria amazonica* lily, 1854

permanent transition between different bodies: this is what challenges the definition of species as self-determined entities. The National Institutes of Health Human Microbiome Project determines that every human body contains more than 10,000 different species of microbe, including bacteria, viruses and fungi, that make up the human microbiome. Humans do not exist as zipped-up and self-defined biology. The human is a collective and ecosystemic condition shaped by flows as a transitioning and non-autonomous enactment. As Jack Halberstam explains, the notion of *transness* needs to be placed within a new biopolitical regime that understands sociability as emerging from the way life transitions interdependently through multiple forms of life and technology.[6] Design intervenes in this transitioning. Design is the medium by which agency unfolds in the biopolitical regime of transness. Life results from this never-concluding transitioning. However, human consciousness does not provide humans with the awareness of the full relational extension of human bodies, nor of the ecosystemic condition of life itself. Design has the capacity to influence, reorient, repair, dramatise and complicate the domain of human consciousness. It can affect the way that human consciousness allows humans to sense their bodies, their ecological condition, and the agency that other entities have in shaping their physicality and metabolisms. Acknowledging the agency of others (and, furthermore, creating the conditions for more-than-human agencies to participate in the outcome of transitioning) is the crucial difference in the cosmopolitical regimes that trans-species architecture contributes to. Ultimately, an architecture that operates from a trans-species perspective establishes more symmetrical conditions for how human and more-than-human entities contribute to the creation of living togetherness. Trans-species architecture confronts the main ecological principle of modernity: its commitment to empower the zipped-up Western man,[7] and its intersection with colonial, carbonising, racialising, technocratic and patriarchal paradigms.

As part of our project Phantom: Mies as Rendered Society (2010), we researched the transformation of the ponds in the reconstruction of Mies's German National Pavilion in Barcelona. The reconstruction had introduced a conventional chlorine-based depuration system that kept the pond water clear at the expense of killing the presence of other forms of life, including the water lilies that Mies and Lilly Reich included in their original design. Twelve years later, not only the lilies but also the flies, the water striders and the fireflies are back, following a long process of transformation and our collaboration with the Fundació Mies van der Rohe, the biologist Carles Palau and many others.[8] It required the transformation of the depuration system, but also important changes in how the pavilion would be taken care of and closer coordination with the city's parks department. Most architects would perceive no change in the pavilion. But its cosmopolitical composition, and its daily production as a human and more-than-human ecology, has been radically reset.

Trans-species architecture is an architecture that, by necessity, operates at connecting scales – it is trans-scalar. In the past, it was thought that architecture operated at the scale of buildings, while industrial design worked at a smaller scale, and urbanism at the larger scale of the metropolis. From the perspective of trans-species architecture, none of those definitions work. Architecture gains its political agency in the transitioning across scales. For instance, microscopic algae floating in the ocean determine the levels of oxygen within the atmosphere, which affects planetary global warming. The microbiological determines and is determined by the planetary. Collective existence affects and is affected by how doors are placed in a building. How thin layers of stone protect bacteria from solar radiation is crucial for humans planning the colonisation of Mars. Architecture and the disputes it is part of are intrinsically trans-scalar.

Architectural agency is in its trans-scalarity. Trans-scalarity is not the same as the interscalar or the multiscalar universality that modernity claimed. The film *Powers of Ten* by Charles and Ray Eames presented the fantasy of a set of distinct scales, from a picnic blanket in a park to a planet floating in space. The film took the perspective, and the authority, of a homogenous, cis, Western and human-centred 'we'. But, in fact, trans-scalarities are always in the making, because they are disputed, divided, accidental, built in difference and messiness.[9] Architecture's agency is embedded in its capacity to exceed scale-containment. Architecture lies in the way gatherings of different entities that operate in different temporal and spatial arrangements – the time and spatiality of infrastructures, the instantaneousness and the microscopic scale of intercellular and molecular action, the latency of online transcontinental transmission, the slow time and territorial scale of geological change and violence[10] – negotiate their mutual

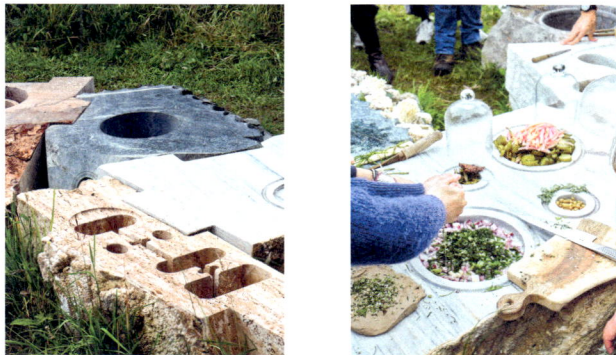

Office for Political Innovation, *The Transspecies Kitchen*, 2021

co-production. To see architecture in this way is not to undermine architectural objecthood. On the contrary, it is from this perspective that the critical dimension of object-production – the effects that form leaves in its wake – can be most clearly understood. The material specificity of buildings is crafted in their entanglement with others. The concreteness of architectural objecthood is both environmental and biopolitical.

Buildings are the product of, and produce, multiple layers of assemblage. Architecture is the assemblage of radically diverse domains. These assemblages are not universal, global or consensual but rather multiple, partial, disconnected from one another, overlapping. They are shaped by dealignment, dispute and disobedience. The heterogeneity and non-universality of trans-species architecture and its enactments make its practice one of dissent and messiness. This dissent can be found in its refusal of the binary of the local and global, the built and the so-called 'natural', the human and non-human. More-than-human architecture is the knowledge of how naive binarism is.

It is precisely at the scales that tend to be invisible to architects (the microscopic and the planetary, the superfast and the superslow) that the presents and futures of existence are now being disputed. Trans-species architecture multiplies the thresholds of architectural consciousness so that design can challenge the way colonisation, carbonisation and anthropocentrism have been concealed on the scalar spectrum. Trans-scalar architecture operates in the domains where humans negotiate with the microbiological, the mineral, the geopolitical, the climatic, the technological and the eco-systemic. It disobeys linear narratives of happy endings, it sidesteps the rhetoric of problems and solutions, and it confronts the fiction that 'the social' is a space of easy agreement. Embracing the multiplicity of architecture's scales and domains is a first step in rebelling against techno-determinism to reset design practices as techno-social. Architecture is not about space, nor about containment. It is not possible for architecture spatially to contain the trans-scalar compositions where life and politics happen. As the eco-social setting where more-than-human messiness takes place, architecture does not operate as a special container but rather as both assembler and assemblage. Architecture does not accommodate or give shelter to the social. Architecture is the rearticulated eco-social.

One way to think about these encounters with non-human life is through cooking. In the Transspecies Kitchen, we explored the way that cooking, digesting, growing and decomposing are all the same: an alliance between different forms of life. Cooking is the externalising of digestion as a collective process of trans-species life-making. Fermenting, in particular, is evidence of the impossibility of individual life. Yoghurt, sauerkraut, cheese, sourdough, dill pickles, cider vinegar, kefir, beer, wine – these alliances are humanly sensed as taste, smell, intoxication, euphoria, sleepiness, drowsiness, dyspepsia, flatulence, diarrhoea, heartburn, acidity, intolerance. Kitchening is a way to increase the collectiveness of intestines. The Transspecies Kitchen that the Office for Political Innovation launched in 2021 is not fuelled by gas, nor by electricity. Instead of transforming animal and vegetal fluids and tissues by heating them, it just nurtures the material interaction of the ecologies within them. It provides the infra-structure and conditions for processes of fermentation to multiply. The shapes carved in the stones and their various degrees of porosity, provide a broad spectrum of conditions so that different living conditions support the diversification of processes where living matter transforms, in a way that is both microscopic, bodily, landscaped and planetary. It is thought of as a microbe–planetary trans-scalar architecture. In the way it operates through processes of fermentation, this kitchen operates similarly to how intestines work. It is conceived as a collective intestine that shows that digestion is not an autonomous process that engages only human bodies. Here, metabolism is a collectively constituted process dependent on other-than-human alliances. The Transspecies Kitchen dilutes the boundaries between cooking, eating and decomposing, which comprise a continuum of molecular progression.

How does this kind of kitchen thinking manifest itself at the scale of the building? The construction of the Reggio School in 2022 outside Madrid allowed us to take further many of our previous ideas and architectural strategies. The design of Reggio School is based on the idea that architectural environments work together with children's bodies and neuronal systems to trigger a desire for exploration and inquiry. In this way, the building is thought of as a complex ecosystem that makes it possible for students to direct their own education through a process of self-driven collective experimentation – following pedagogical ideas that Loris Malaguzzi

Office for Political Innovation, Reggio School, Madrid, 2022

and parents in the Italian city of Reggio Emilia developed to empower children's capacity to deal with unpredictable challenges and possibilities.

Reggio School is a living ecosystem that contributes to caring for the larger earth-system of the Madrid district of Valdebebas and multiplying its biodiversity. Collecting rainfall and distributing it through the building, the school nurtures tiny gardens within its architecture. These have been carefully designed so that the plants and insects lost to decades of pesticide and fertiliser used in neighbouring suburban lots grow and expand from them, empowering the life and diversity of the larger territory the school is part of.

In the context of southern Europe, where high-tech sustainable solutions are only available to high-budget, corporate or state-promoted buildings, this building develops a low-budget strategy to reduce its environmental footprint based on the following design principles:

1. Reggio School is a compact vertical building, as opposed to most schools, which have large footprints. Minimising the building's footprint reduces the need for foundations, and makes the building more compact and therefore more energy-efficient.

2. It radically reduces standard construction elements. There is no cladding, no drop ceilings, no raised technical floors, no wall linings, no ventilated facades. The amount of material used in the facades, roofs and interior partitions of the building has been reduced by 48% just by replacing a big part of the construction by means of simple strategies for thermal insulation and mechanical system distribution. The result presents a naked building, where the visibility of its operating components defines its aesthetics.

3. It has a thick wrapping of living insulation. The cork facade provides both thermal insulation and support for more-than-human life. Eighty per cent of the building's envelope is covered by a 14cm-deep layer of cork. This natural material not only reduces the school's energy consumption by 50%, its irregular surface allows organic material to accumulate so that the facade will eventually become the habitat of numerous forms of microbiological fungi and vegetal and animal life.

The design, construction and use of this building is intended to move beyond 'sustainable architecture' to engage with ecology as a holistic perspective. Here, more-than-human alliances, materials, collective governance and education intersect through architecture. Avoiding homogenisation and unified standards, the architecture of the school aims to become a multiverse where the layered complexity of the environment becomes readable and experiential. It operates as an assemblage of different climates, ecosystems, architectural traditions and regulations. This is a form of practice that is making its way amid the cracks of a modern legacy that is no longer capable of responding to the ecological, climatic and societal crisis that modernity triggered. In this form of practice, our office is one in permanent interaction with other architectural firms around the world. This network of interlocutors includes Takk, The Living, SCAPE, ANAcycle, Mio Tsuneyama, Fuminori Nousaku Architects, Boonserm Premthada, Yussef Agbo-Ola, Cooking Sections, C+ arquitectas and elii. As I write this text, we are all working on projects where architecture needs to play a role that goes beyond sustainability. These are projects that share an architectural approach that understands how reality is made of the interaction of very diverse presences and processes. In the work of these offices, architecture is more-than-human architecture. It is a trans-species, transmaterial and trans-scalar architecture. Architecture faces the vertigo of losing its role in surrounding voids, and the trauma of finding out that space was never empty. Of finding out that there was never a beginning or an end to construction, and that human design negotiates with that of others. But what we find under the umbrella of trans-species architecture is making architecture needed and relevant: it expands our sensing capacity and provides a planetary and microbial dimension to our bodies. It is definitively a different era for architecture, and one where the current climate and ecological crisis opens alternative political, aesthetic and scientific forms of life, and therefore forms of being social.

1. Ivan L. Munuera, 'Cactus Obsession', *Journal of Architectural Education* 77/2 (2023), 209–25.
2. Isabelle Stengers, *Cosmopolitics I*, trans. Robert Bononno (Minneapolis: University of Minnesota Press, 2011).
3. Tatiana Holway, *The Flower of Empire: an Amazonian Water Lily, the Quest to Make it Bloom, and the World it Created* (New York: Oxford University Press, 2013).
4. Andrés Jaque, 'Mies in the basement: the ordinary confronts the exceptional in the Barcelona pavilions', *Thresholds* 43 (2015): 120–278.
5. Dan Handl, *Designed Forests: A Cultural History* (Milton Park, Oxfordshire: Routledge, 2015).
6. Jack Halberstam, *Trans*: A Quick and Quirky Account of Gender Variability* (Oakland: University of California Press, 2018).
7. Rosi Braidotti asks who is the *anthro* of anthropocentrism, and characterises it as the Western white colonial subject, in Rosi Braidotti, *The Posthuman* (Cambridge: Polity Press, 2013).
8. They included the Municipal Institute of Parks and Gardens of Barcelona, the Botanical Garden of Barcelona, the Biennial of Landscape Architecture, Aleksandra Kędziorek, and Małgorzata Kuciewicz and Simone De Iacobis
9. Andrés Jaque, *Superpowers of Scale* (New York: Columbia Books on Architecture and the City, 2020).
10. Rob Nixon, *Slow Violence and the Environmentalism of the Poor* (Cambridge: Harvard University Press, 2013).

Living materials:
from the geological to the metabolic

Jia Yi Gu

In 1738, a duck defecated and set in motion a dynamic debate in Western thought on the distinction between the living and the non-living.[1] This particular duck was not 'alive'. Instead, it was a mechanical duck engineered by Jacques de Vaucanson, the son of a Grenoble glove-maker, to simulate the organic processes of an animal feeding, including the acts of digestion and defecation.[2] Vaucanson's duck claimed to be a machine that moved itself and digested for itself.[3] Its virtuosity in metabolic processing – or animacy – was read as a sign of life, transforming French philosophical debates on the very principles that separated the living from the non-living. Vaucanson's automaton forced French natural philosophers to confront the possibility that non-living things could one day simulate living functions, thus collapsing the natural with the artificial.

In the present day, a parallel convergence is occurring between the authorial hand of the maker and mimetic acts of nature.[4] Contemporary designers are no longer imitating natural processes: they are working with living materials in ways that set those processes in motion. They are authoring the life cycles of living organisms and guiding metabolic flows. In swapping mechanical life for the biological, new modes of thought are emerging to complicate long-standing divisions between living and non-living, between the natural and the artificial, between the designer as author and as collaborator.

What does it mean to 'work with nature'? To co-design with the animal, or the microorganism? How do you guide a material with a life form of its own? When does discovered biology become manufactured technology? What new ethics are required as designers investigate the possibilities of incorporating living systems as materials? In these new practices of tending, what is the boundary between *gardening* and *agriculture* – between the intimate and domestic act of cultivating, and the industrialised practices of food production?[5] When is it cooperation and when extraction?[6]

Nearly all material objects of everyday life are touched by petroleum, a fuel that comes from the Earth's crust. This liquid is formed from the remains of once living organisms, including animals, plants, algae and bacteria. Of the materials spanning our building sites to our desktops, nearly all are derived from or dependent on the global petrochemical pipeline transforming fossilised dead matter into end product. This transformation is a chemical one, beginning with the processing of fossil fuels into raw materials, or chemical 'feedstock', which in turn are converted into polymers and intermediary chemical components. These are then manufactured into materials utilised in all manner of products including foams, dyes, adhesives, soap, paints, fibres and plastic itself. From the extraction of raw matter to the processing of chemical feedstock, nearly all materials of everyday life are sourced from or supplemented by this pipeline. Once considered to be a 'modern' and efficient method of production, the resource-intensive processes of extracting, processing, producing and distributing materials are contributing to global ecological breakdown. The environmental degradation we are experiencing today, in the form of exponential wildfires and rapid flooding, winter heatwaves and historical droughts, are the direct result of the century-long dependency on environmentally harmful material processes.

Current approaches to reducing the environmental impact of materials are often firmly focused on substituting plasticated stock for 'natural' matter – for example, replacing the inventory of single-use plastic spoons with wooden or bamboo-derived compostable material. Substituting or exchanging non-degradable source matter for renewable matter is a positive step in reducing domestic landfill, but is it sufficient? From the perspective of designers of living systems, such approaches simply mirror the extractive model for traditional materials and the linear flow of energy transforming source matter into product. Replacing the dead matter of petrochemical (plastic) with the once-living matter of wood fibres fails to dismantle the habits of extraction required to make the material substrates of our lives.

Contemporary researchers and practitioners are seeking alternatives to non-renewable systems by attending to regenerative processes found in living systems. These experimental practices incorporate the activities of living organisms, such as cells, bacteria, yeast, algae and fungi, into material fabrication. This science of redirecting metabolic life towards human use is an emergent and growing field, with applications across diverse sectors, among them the medical sciences, energy studies and agriculture. From the cultivation of faux meat to the conversion of algae into fuel, from the cellulose growth of SCOBY (a naturally occurring and edible culture found in kombucha) to the printing of human organs, the incorporation of non-human, living systems into human material processes is reorienting design's relationship to matter and to nature. Rather than imitating nature, designers are creating conditions conducive to natural life. From a linear operation to a circular one, from inert matter to active systems, the materials of design have shifted, as has the definition of the designer and their labour.

The conversion of metabolic life into human use transforms the activities of the designer from *making* to *growing*. Feeding, cultivating and tending become the primary acts of the designer, and human and animal co-perform and co-produce in the making of material things. In parallel, new sites

Jacques de Vaucanson, *Canard Digérateur* (Digesting Duck), 1739

of production emerge in the interdisciplinary work of making with living systems. The studio is replaced by a clinical laboratory, the workshop with a plant nursery, the desktop with a wet aquarium, and the library with a soil repository. The seamstress works alongside the biologist to develop material processes utilising living, non-human agents, culminating in the forms of bacterial colonies, rooting scaffolds and slumbering mycelium.

In their laboratory, bio-textile designers Faber Futures seek to replace traditional dying processes with microbial dyes, incorporating the metabolic processes of bacterial colonies into wearable textiles. Textile processes cause the most ecological harm during the finishing and dying stages because of intensive water usage and heavily polluting petroleum-based dyes. Rather than derive pigmentation from fossilised forms, Faber Futures harness the living processes of the soil-dwelling bacterium *Streptomyces coelicolor*.

93

The scientific name of *Streptomyces coelicolor* illustrates the unique qualities that were apparent when it was discovered – the term *coelicolor* is Latin for colour of the sky or heaven. *S. coelicolor* is a multicellular mycelial bacteria that can be monitored and modified to cling to dyed textiles. Under the right conditions, the bacteria secretes an antibiotic to fight infection. The antibiotic emits a pigment molecule, which, depending on its nutrient sources, produces colour. The colours in the pigment molecules – for example, blue or red – are emitted by metabolites, or small molecules, as a sort of microbial defence. In other words, the pigments can be understood as a process of repair. Thus, in working with bacterial colonies, Faber Futures are challenging the non-regenerative dying practices of fast fashion, while harnessing the repair practices of bacterial forms.

Naturally recurring cycles of growth and decay offer alternatives to the exploitation of non-renewable resources, as biological resources can be returned to the Earth or fed back into other organic cycles, hinting towards a future of ecological repair in architecture and design. Often described as 'automatic' or 'self-occurring', activities of living materials are understood as self-directed by organisms that exhibit *autopoiesis*, or the ability to regenerate and maintain themselves (reproduction and maintenance are the core of their labour). Living systems produce their own components, but also assemble and reassemble them in ways that ensure their own future existence (in contrast to mechanical assemblages, which do not have the capacity to reproduce their own components). In these processes, the designer is deploying biologically occurring processes. Does that mean that authorship is shared with the material? Certainly, the outcome cannot be fully controlled – or 'designed'. Who is directing whom?

Accalmie is a table made of slumbering mycelium, the root-like structure of fungus. Designed by Corentin Mahieu, Bento Architecture and Sonian (a designer, an architecture office and a cooperative, respectively), Accalmie is constructed with a wooden structural scaffold as its base and a stabilised body of mycelium as its surface. The beechwood for the scaffold is sourced from an eighteenth-century timber farm in the Sonian Forest, a 5,000-acre beech forest that has been designated as a UNESCO World Heritage Site. The tabletop is formed of a species of mycelium collected from the same beech forest, where it grows naturally. The mycelium is cultivated on a substrate formed of the waste wood material. In turn, the network of fungi is suspended, slowing its growth in unfavourable conditions, and ready to resume growth when reactivated in its preferred environment. In the slumbering mycelium, how do we understand or articulate the relationship between the designer and the designed object? Are designers domesticating or co-performing with their living agents? Is the mycelium sleeping or was it put to sleep? Who determines its awakening?

There are many terms used to describe the process of crafting with living materials: biomaterials, biosystems, biotechnology, biological engineering, bio-based, biofabrication, living systems, regenerative design. As terms proliferate, so too do scales of operation. Working with living media and their life cycles offers a critical step towards regenerative systems; the domestication of living beings also produces a 'synthetic biology', a discipline that seeks to customise biological systems engineered towards precision, according to human definitions. It is the act of transforming an ancient art – domestication of animal life – into a contemporary and ethical practice.

How do living systems represent themselves? How do designers, operating within the boundaries of our human sensorium, come to know living organisms? What is knowable to us, as humans, when we perceive colour in bacteria? Working with living systems that confound human perception, such as mycelia and bacteria, invites questions around the ordering of knowledge itself, about the limits of knowing. As the term 'more-than-human' proliferates, the original idea – a challenge to human perception –

Bento Architecture, the making of *Accalmie*, 2023–24

risks being lost. Beyond the harnessing of microbial, algal and fungal forms, the term 'more-than-human' questioned the human sensorium as a primary mode of inquiry for designers, so that we might acquire the temporal sensibilities of a sequoia; the spatial sensibilities of air; the colour theories of bacteria.[7]

How is the material world conceived, how is it ordered, and on which living systems? Questions of life and the boundaries between *living* and *non-living*, between *human* and *more-than-human*, thus abound in the metabolic experiments of contemporary designers. Like the mechanical defecating duck, the automation of living systems seems to be proof of their autonomy, outside of human design. From the pigmentation of dying bacteria to the slumbering of mycelium slabs, nature (and its processes) appears as just is. In reproducing systems 'found' in nature, the authorial hand of the designer is absent in the medium but present in the making. The distance between designer and matter seems to be collapsing. Matter is both directed and automated, feeding and being fed. The designer is alive, along with her material – and so a kinship seems possible. Yet how closely, or correctly, or ethically can human designers work with and make from the metabolic life of the non-human? What is their relationship to the lives they are tending? In celebrating the circularity of metabolic systems, which grow, die and grow again, are designers feeding life or augmenting death? Are they harnessing 'natural' processes or subsuming biological processes to technical control? Is it gardening or is it agriculture?

1. This historical anecdote is indebted to Jessica Riskin's history of Vaucanson's duck in 'The Defecating Duck, or, the ambiguous origins of artificial life', *Critical Inquiry* 29/4 (2003), 599–633.

2. While self-operating machines were known in this period, most automata imitated observable actions in animal behaviour: for example, the flapping of a wing or the turn of a head.

3. The imitation was internal, not external, mirroring to the unobservable functioning of the animal rather than observable expressions of animal behaviour, and dramatises the distance between mechanism and imitation. See Riskin, 12.

4. See Lorraine Daston, 'Representation to presentation', in Lorraine Daston and Peter L. Galison, *Objectivity* (Brooklyn, New York: Zone Books, 2010), 363.

5. This question is posed by art historian Caroline A. Jones in 'Conversation: Assia Crawford, Maru Garcia, and Caroline A. Jones on feeding', in Kate Yeh Chiu and Jia Yi Gu (eds.), *Material Acts: Experimentation in Architecture and Design* (Los Angeles: Craft Contemporary, 2024).

6. The term 'more-than-human' has evolved from its introduction by cultural ecologist David Abram nearly thirty years ago. In his book *The Spell of the Sensuous: Perception and Language in a More-Than-Human World* (New York: Vintage Books, 1997), the the term is offered as an alternative to human modes of knowledge production — as a critique of the representation of nature through systems of abstraction and inscription, such as alphabetic writing. Abram questioned the human sensorium and the legitimacy of one sensorial experience presiding over the production and governance of knowledge, and guiding our relationship with a thing called nature.

7. See Caroline Jones, 'A common sense: a conversation with Caroline A. Jones', transcript of conversation from 15 March 2018, on *Edge*, https://www.edge.org/conversation/caroline_a_jones-a-common-sense [Accessed 4 April 2025].

These two headpieces were created by two distinct Indigenous communities: the Bororo in Brazil, and the Macushi, in Guyana. However, they share an approach to the use of materials that is sympathetic, rather than extractive. Plant fibres for the woven structure were sourced locally and mature feathers were collected when they were shed by the bird, rather than plucked. As a result, these impressive objects have been made with minimal harm to the maker's environment.

Unknown maker, Coronet of parrot feathers, c. 1905
Opposite: Unknown maker, Headpiece with feathers, c. 1958

For thousands of years, humans have relied on animals for labour or food, often at the expense of the animal's wellbeing. In some cases, we have bred them to become dependent on us. Humans have a duty of care for these animals, and societies the world over have developed ways to make them more comfortable. The objects on display here were made in the UK, Japan, Kenya and South Sudan.

Above: Unknown maker, Horse sandals, c. 1909
Below: Unknown maker, Surrogate calf, c. 1978
Opposite: Unknown maker, Hobble boots, twentieth century

This might mean protecting their hooves with hobble-boots or sandals, building a hive with windows to check on bees without disturbing them, or providing a surrogate to comfort animals whose offspring have been removed. Favoured animals may also receive special treatment, like a special collar.

George Neighbour and Sons, Skep hive, unknown date
Opposite above: H.B. Lucas, Dummy eggs, unknown date
Opposite below: Unknown maker, Collar for favourite bull calf, early twentieth century

For over two decades, architects Cesare Leonardi and Franca Stagi documented trees across the world to produce this collection of 374 drawings. Their research stemmed from a conviction that, to design a thriving park, one must have a thorough knowledge of trees. Leonardi made scale drawings of each species to understand their forms and variations and thus centre their needs. The tree species shown here grow immediately around the Design Museum and in Holland Park.

Cesare Leonardi, Franca Stagi, Common hornbeam (*Carpinus betulus*) ard Pin oak (*Quercus palustris*) from *L'Architettura degli Alberi* (The Architecture of Trees) series, 1962–82

Traditional fish traps are examples of designs that embody more-than-human relationships. They employ natural materials, are reusable, and minimise the impact of human needs on other species. These traps are carefully constructed to fit the adults of a particular species and allow young fish to escape. They are left in moving water to trap the fish, rather than dragging nets through water or along the seabed. This guarantees future catches and the survival of the species that humans rely on to feed themselves. This group of baskets includes examples from England, Guyana, Myanmar and Tanzania.

Ivor Cadogan, Salmon trap, 1964
Opposite, clockwise from top left: Unknown maker, Fish trap, early twentieth century;
Stanley Bird, Eel trap, mid-twentieth century; Unknown maker, Fish trap, early twentieth
century; Unknown maker, Fish trap model, nineteenth century

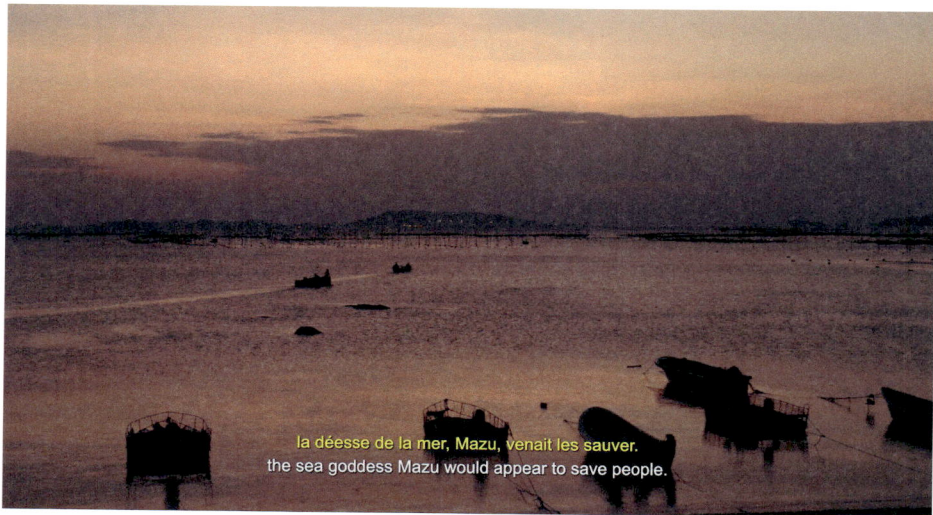

la déesse de la mer, Mazu, venait les sauver.
the sea goddess Mazu would appear to save people.

In 2022, Beijing-based DnA Architecture were invited to submit a design for a museum on the island of Meizhou in Fujian Province, China. Instead, they proposed subtle interventions on six sites around the island, each of which supports different activities and species. Repurposing existing materials and structures wherever possible, the project is a blueprint for having a minimal impact on ecosystems and promoting the regeneration of multiple species, as seen in the videos.

en parcourant l'île entière.
我们对整座小岛的调查是一步一步走出来的

DnA Architecture, *Into the Island*, 2022–ongoing

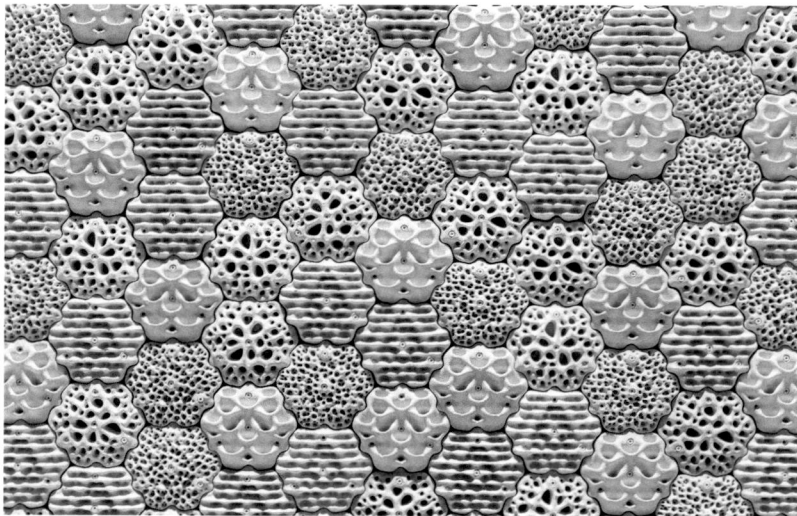

Coral reef destruction is a tangible consequence of climate change and intensive fishing. MARS II exemplifies how design can play a decisive role in its regeneration. This structure is composed of 3D-printed modular units that can be deployed from small boats and slotted onto a metal scaffold on the seabed, without the need for barges or cranes. The creviced surface of each module supports both transplanted and naturally occurring coral. The artificial reef also shelters fish.

Reef Design Lab, *Modular Artificial Reef Structure (MARS) II*, 2023
Opposite: Reef Design Lab, *Living Seawall panels*, 2018

This project began as a response to the damage to human infrastructure and coastal ecosystems caused by Hurricane Sandy across the Caribbean and coastal United States in 2012. SCAPE designed a number of modules for the breakwaters that are being built off the coast of Staten Island in New York. This artificial structure will defend against coastal erosion, provide a habitat for a variety of marine species, and be the focus for education programmes in the region. It is part of the Billion Oyster Project, which aims to rebuild and repopulate New York Harbor's oyster reefs.

Kate Orff/SCAPE, *Living Breakwaters*, 2025
Overleaf: detail of a breakwater module

Weald to Waves is one of many initiatives in the UK seeking to address the loss of biodiversity in our countryside. In order to thrive, species need space to roam, locate food and find shelter. This project is connecting landowners, landscape architects, scientists and communities across Sussex in a common goal: to create a 100-mile-long wildlife corridor.

Video stills from *Weald to Waves*, 2022–ongoing

This pavilion offers shelter to humans, plants, insects and fungi alike. It combines mass-produced insulating bricks with locally sourced clay and wood. The photographs record the original version of the pavilion built in the courtyard between the Museum of Finnish Architecture and the Design Museum in Helsinki. It featured additional panels made of biochar, a charcoal-like fertiliser. Over several seasons, a garden and insect community flourished around the structure, while the architects used the project as a site of experimentation, observation and learning.

Suomi/Koivisto, *Alusta Pavilion*, 2023

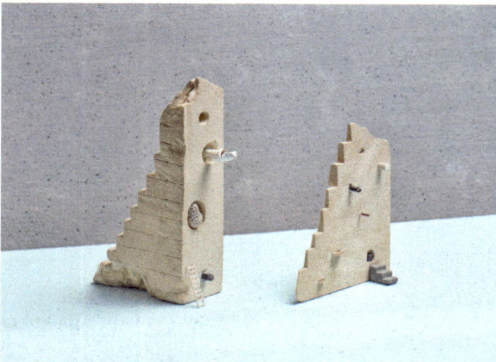

Studio Ossidiana design spaces that encourage encounters between species. For this long-running project, they have researched the architecture of aviaries, pigeon lofts, bat towers, bird feeders, cages and traps. The variety of architectural types expressed in these models, which resemble a city for birds, reflect the different relationships that humans have formed with birds, keeping them as pets, training them to deliver messages, or harvesting their droppings for fertiliser.

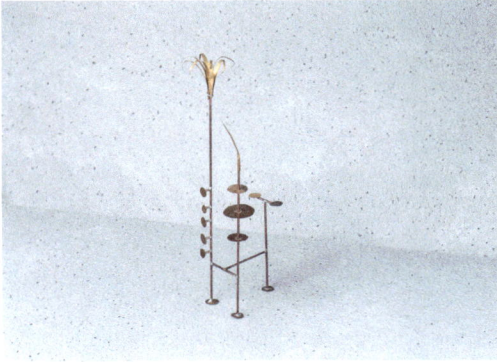

Studio Ossidiana, *The City of Birds*, 2019–22

What does a chair look like when its intended users are insects, not humans? Marlène Huissoud offers an answer through her collaboration with scientists Robert Francis and Brandon Mak. Together, they designed a series of forms, including this chair, which provide habitats for insects such as solitary bees, wasps and butterflies. The size of each hole and the colour of the natural binder applied to the surface have been chosen to provide shelter that will be attractive to these insects.

122

Marlène Huissoud, *The Chair*, 2019

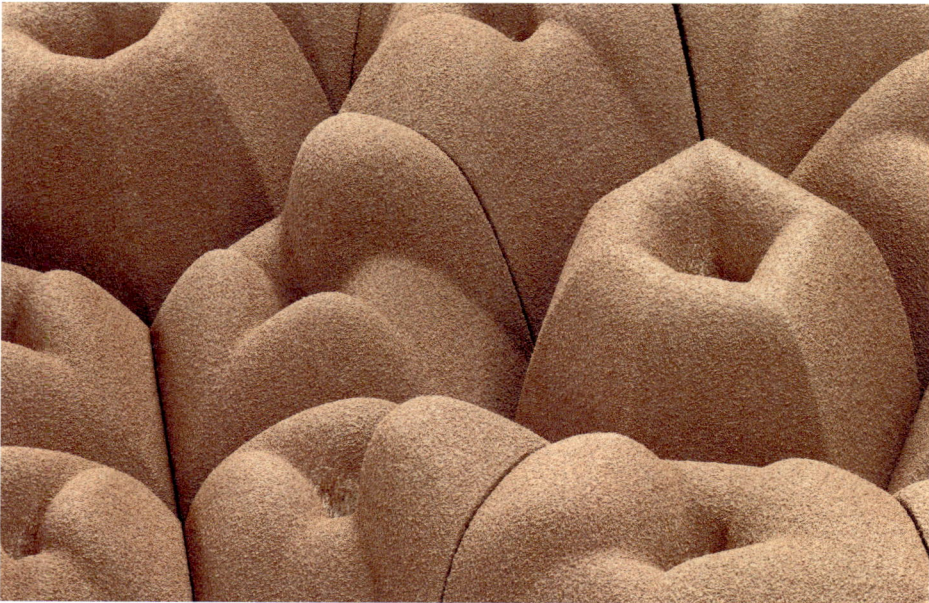

Andrés Jaque envisions architecture as a dynamic, flourishing ecosystem rather than as a static container for people. *The Transspecies Rosette* proposes cladding that is both beautiful and functional, with a more-than-human design that fosters mutually beneficial trans-species relationships. It is composed of ground cork and natural resin, simultaneously providing waterproof insulation for the building and a substrate for other species to grow on, including invisible microbes and fungi.

Andrés Jaque/Office for Political Innovation, *The Transspecies Rosette*, 2025

These building facades have different sized apertures to attract birds or insects. They have been 3D printed using discarded rice husks and recycled glass powder, demonstrating Johanna Seelemann's commitment to reusing waste materials for the benefit of other species. The profiles of the façades have insulating properties that, when applied at scale, may reduce energy consumption. Versions of both façades have been applied to a building in Milan, Italy, to test their efficiency.

Johanna Seelemann, *Habitat* (bird façade), 2024

Johanna Seelemann designed these vases in the shape of petrol cans as a commentary on the competition between plants and cars in urban environments. Made of low-fired terracotta instead of metal, they function as clay pot irrigation systems. This ancient method involves burying a clay pot up to its neck and filling it with water, which leeches out to surrounding plants. This process uses 70% less water than surface irrigation.

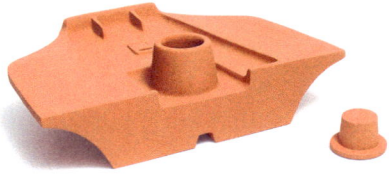

Johanna Seelemann, *Oase* (Oasis) *R1*, *H1*, *K1. W1*, 2023

Although pigeons are mostly perceived as urban pests, humans actually share a history of productive cohabitation with them. Throughout the regions surrounding the Mediterranean, dovecotes have long provided shelter to pigeons and served to collect their guano (excrement), once considered the best agricultural fertiliser. *Dovecote for London* is a design proposal catering both to pigeons' welfare by providing them with a home in the city, and to our needs by supplying guano for urban farms.

James Peplow Powell, *Dovecote for London*, 2023

In the United States, between 100 million and one billion birds die each year from collisions with glazed buildings. This is because they do not see the glass, focusing instead on the habitats it mirrors or encloses. The Bird-Safe Building Guidelines is a freely available publication presenting design solutions to prevent these deadly collisions. The images of affected species are shown here alongside a sample of film that can be applied to glass, ensuring that it becomes non-reflective or patterned to birds.

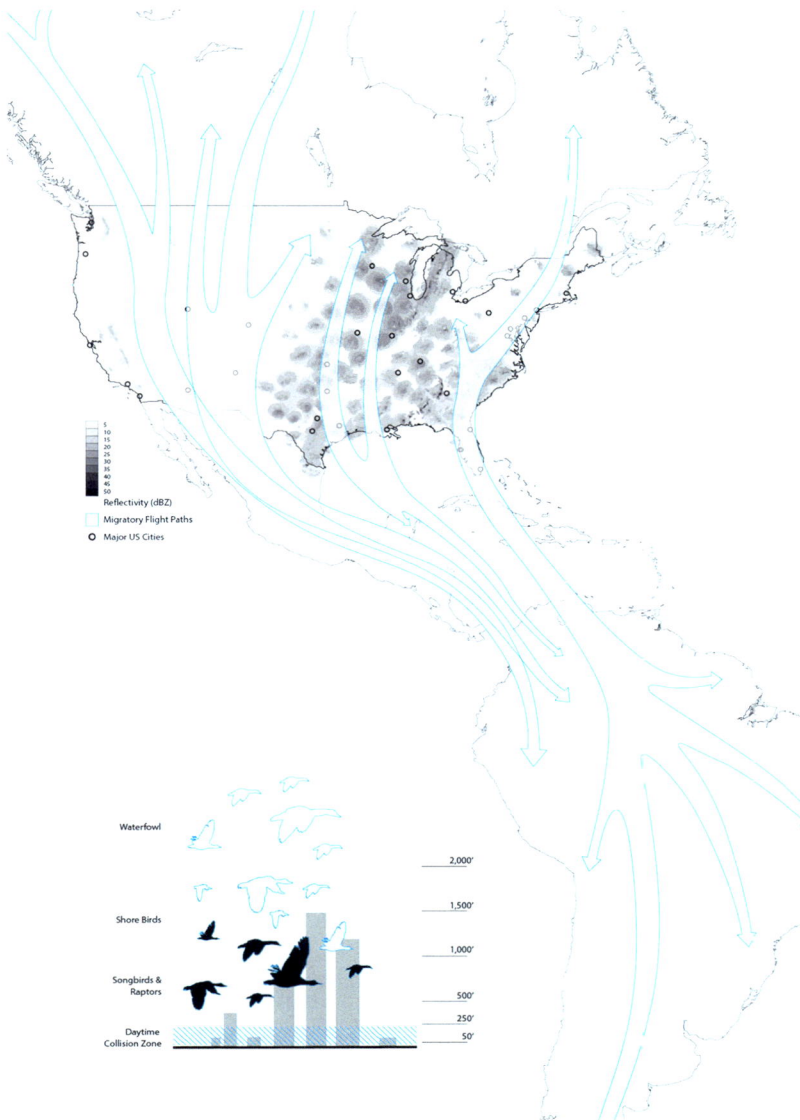

Waterfowl

Shore Birds

Songbirds & Raptors

Daytime Collision Zone

2,000'

1,500'

1,000'

500'

250'

50'

Reflectivity (dBZ)

5
10
15
20
25
30
35
40
45
50

Migratory Flight Paths

Major US Cities

SCAPE Landscape Architecture, *Bird-Safe Building Guidelines*, 2022–25

This table's scaffold-like base was made from Belgian beechwood, while its tabletop was created by growing mycelium – the root-like part of fungi – using waste from the base as a substrate. The same method was applied to produce two accompanying stools. *Accalmie*, which translates as 'lull' or 'calm', refers to the mycelium's state. After rapid growth, it is now dormant, though it can be reactivated for future adaptations or repairs.

Bento Architecture, *Accalmie*, 2023–24

135

These two banners are made by combining red algae and mineral pigments. Jessie French developed this material as an alternative to the single-use vinyl used in window displays. She uses it to highlight different scales of time: the millions of years it takes to form the pigments, the few weeks or months in which algae grow and the many hundreds of years it takes for man-made plastics to decompose.

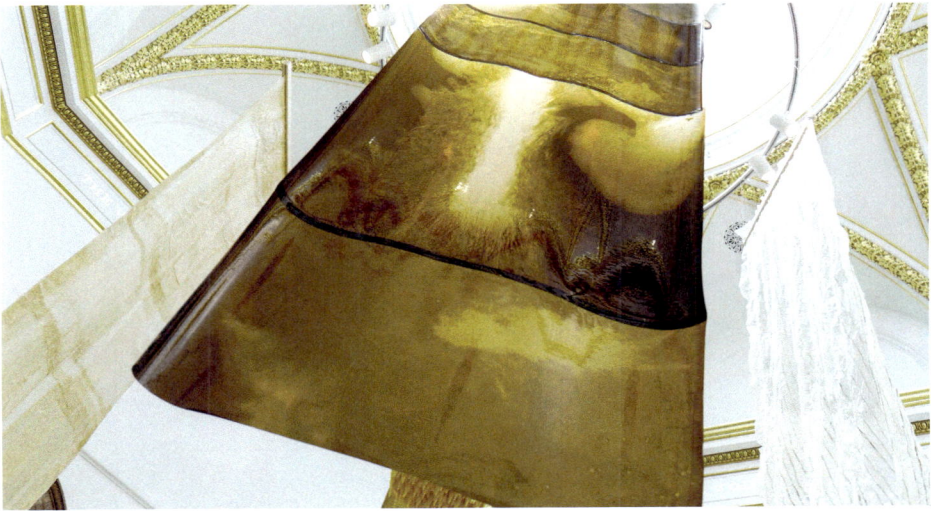

Jessie French, *1708 – Sands of Time, 1707 – Red Flag*, 2024

Faber Futures explore ways of reducing the environmental impact of industrial production. For this jacket, which they produced under their brand Normal Phenomena of Life (NPOL), they applied a bacterium found in soil called *Streptomyces coelicor* to silk. The pigment that it secretes resulted in the swirls, spots and blushes visible on this design. Each garment is unique and requires a fraction of the amount of water needed for conventional dyeing processes.

Faber Futures, NPOL Original Exploring Jacket and Musette, 2023

This monumental wall hanging was not woven but was instead entirely grown out of plant roots. Artist Diana Scherer encourages plants to follow pathways in the structures that she designs, taking inspiration from human traces like car tracks and natural patterns such as tree rings and plant cells. The work offers a glimpse of subterranean networks otherwise invisible to us, revealing their ability to adapt to – and occasionally ignore – frameworks set up by humans.

Diana Scherer, *Apical #6*, 2024
Overleaf: detail

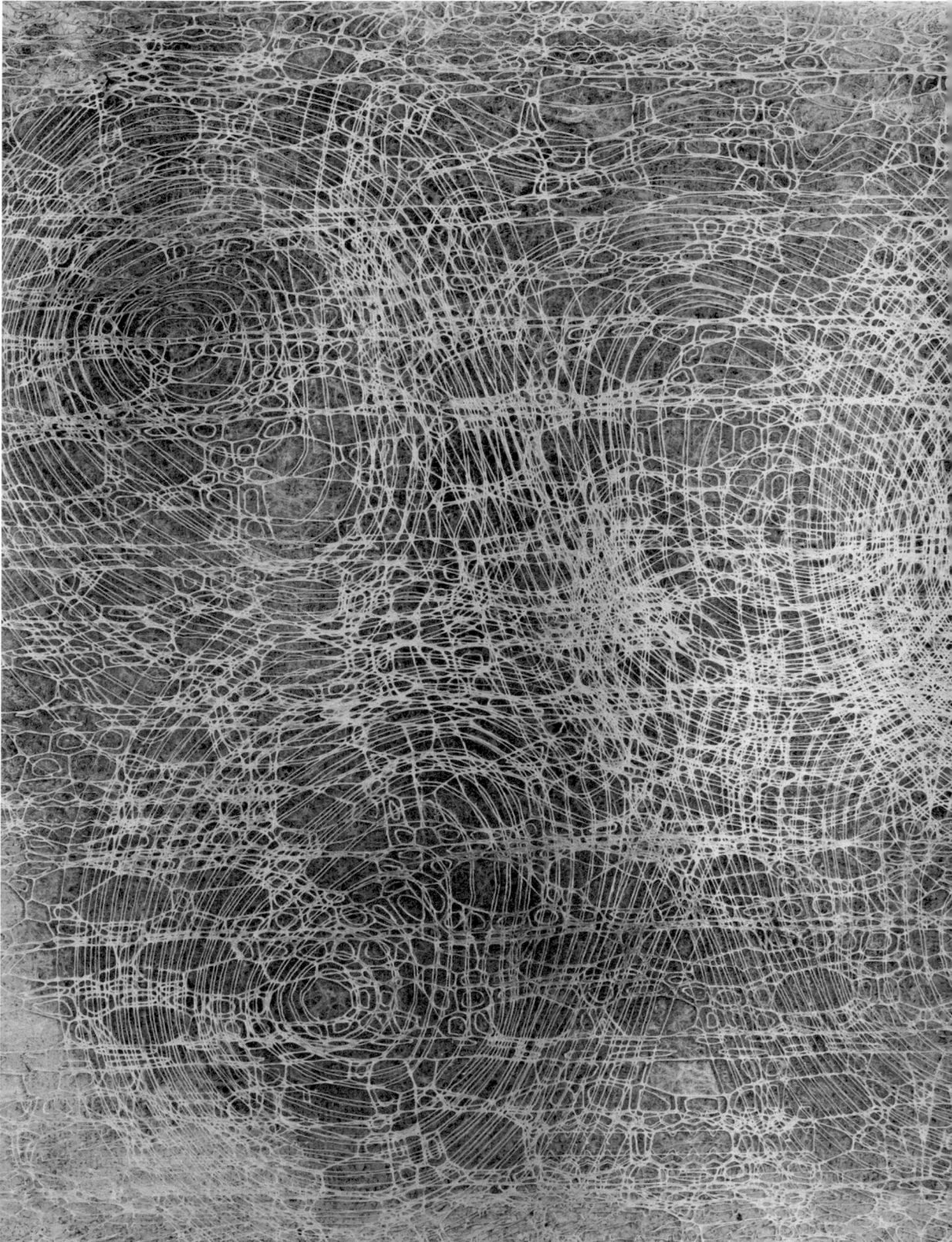

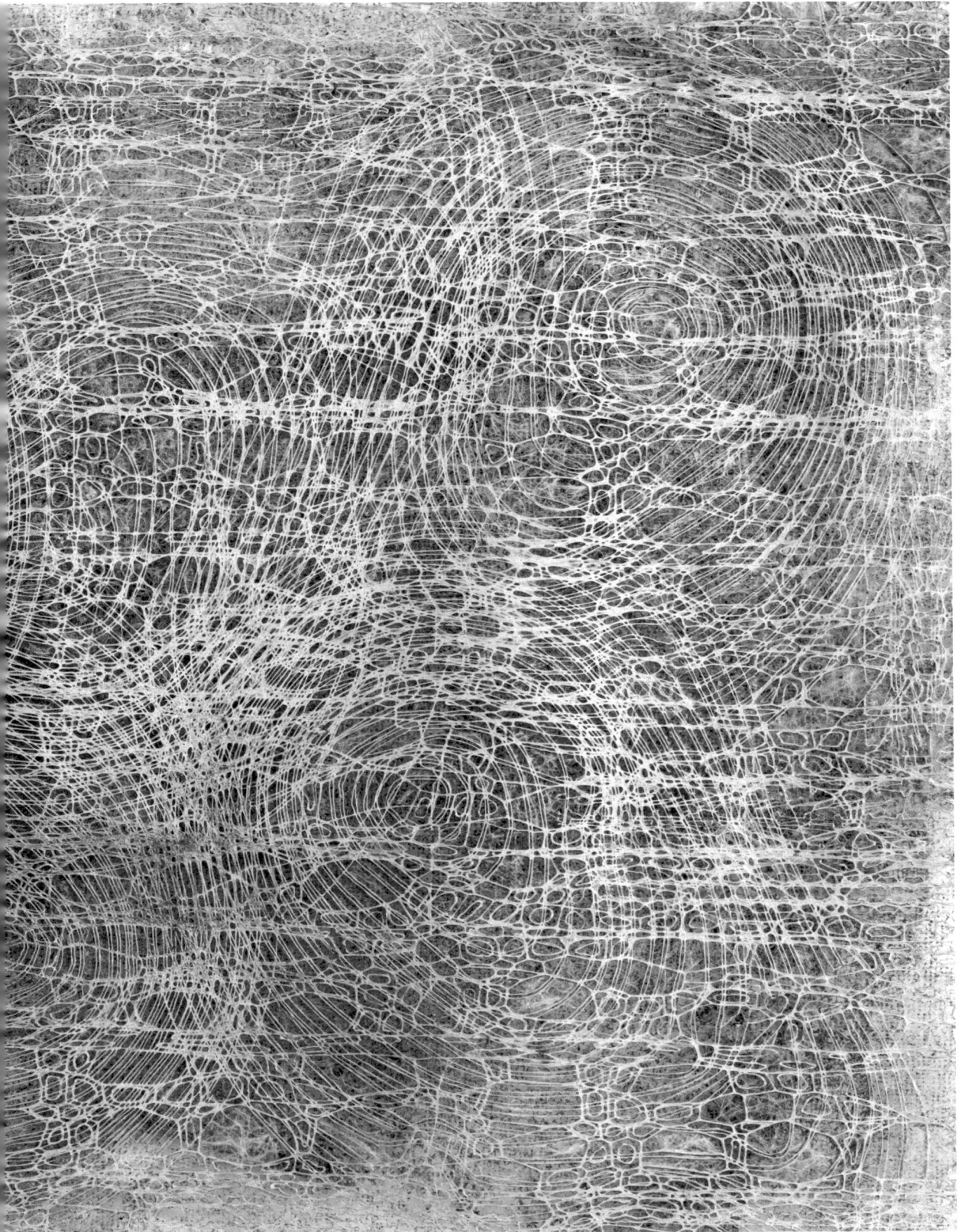

Feifei Zhou, *The Coast Is Not a Line, It's a Zone*, 2025

Contemporary cartography often reduces the coast to a single, unbroken line, oversimplifying a dynamic and complex zone of ecological and social interactions that shape coastal communities. Today, as coastal hardening projects like land reclamation, seawalls, and industrial aquaculture transform the shoreline into a continuous, rigid boundary, we witness the isolation of wet and dry, sea and land. These hardened coasts erase the rich interstitial spaces where marginalized coastal communities and more-than-human lives coexist. To counter the reductive tendencies of maps and coastal hardening projects, for her fellowship, Feifei Zhou asked: How can we reimagine and better understand the coast?

Zhou's project situated itself in Kupang, on Timor Island in Indonesia, and centres around the traditional fishing device known as the *sero* as an example of life-sustaining practices. Crafted from locally sourced materials such as Gewang palm (*Corypha utan Lam.*) leaves and mangrove wood, the *sero* works with the natural rhythms of ocean waves. Its handwoven panels, carefully designed for flexibility across diverse coastal conditions, feature small gaps that allow juvenile fish and shrimp to escape, fostering ecological regeneration. Through drawing, filming and mapmaking, Zhou's work evidences the making, installation and use of the *sero* as a life-sustaining practice for humans and non-humans alike. Zhou's work with local villagers, and her time in Kupang, has led her to extend her work beyond documentation and toward practical intervention and advocacy for the *sero*.

Through ethnographic fieldwork, in collaboration with Gillian Bogart at University of California, Santa Cruz, the research follows the daily routines of fisherfolk in the village of Oli'o, who practice *sero*-based fishing. By recording their spatial movements and activities on day-long fishing and foraging journeys, the project captures a different depiction of the coast – not as a rigid, singular boundary but as a vast, living zone where more-than-human lives are sustained and able to thrive.

More than Human Fellow

A *sero*

Feifei Zhou, *The Coast Is Not a Line, It's a Zone*, 2025
Overleaf: detail from *The Coast Is Not a Line, It's a Zone*, 2025

147

III

Shifting Perspective

Dunne & Raby, *Memento Figure 2*, from *Designs for a World of Many Worlds,
After the Festival*, 2023–24

How does the world look to a dolphin, an insect or a river? The conundrum of a non-human experience has captivated imaginations since antiquity. Today, we are rediscovering our interdependence with more-than-human lives, and turning to speculation to understand and empathise with their needs. While we will never truly know what it's like to be another species, embracing this cognitive leap allows us to imagine, and appreciate, worldviews other than our own.

Shifting our perspective is a step towards recognising the breadth and complexity of non-human intelligences, addressing their needs and even honouring their pleasure. But how to do so? Some contemporary practitioners turn to technology to explore the subjectivities of natural bodies, such as by training an AI model to speak on behalf of a polluted river. Others employ play as a tool to stretch our subjecthood beyond our bodies, using costuming and props to embody other species – play is, after all, a serious mode of inquiry. In this chapter, designers Anthony Dunne and Fiona Raby encourage the expansion of design's imaginative capacity by 'wrestling with the unthinkable' and celebrating the alienness of the non-human. Meanwhile, interdisciplinary researcher Michelle Westerlaken traces a history of more-than-human design practices, assessing their efficacy in generating truly equitable multispecies relationships.

By featuring works made by, with or for other species, this chapter invites us to expand the parameters of what we consider design. The works represented focus on decentering our needs and rethinking our place in the world through experiments in kinship and coexistence with other forms of life. This repositioning is not an end in itself, but ultimately – as the effects of climate change intensify – a strategy for survival.

Margherita Dosi Delfini

Inviting multispecies proposals

Michelle Westerlaken

In retrospect, 1974 and 1975 turned out to be two crucial years for more-than-human design. Architecture and media collective Ant Farm proposed the construction of An Embassy to the Dolphins, a speculative research station to study human–dolphin social relations and envision multispecies futures.[1] At the same time, evolutionary biologist Lynn Margulis and Earth scientist James Lovelock published their Gaia hypothesis, positing that Earth's living and non-living entities interact as a system to maintain conditions conducive to life.[2] Margulis dedicated her career to developing the theory of evolutionary symbiosis, the by now widely accepted idea that life did not take over the Earth by combat but by networking.[3] Meanwhile, ethicist Peter Singer published his book *Animal Liberation*, an important work for the growing animal rights movement that would popularise the notion of speciesism to refer to the exploitation of and discrimination against other animals by humans.[4] Finally, philosopher Thomas Nagel's essay 'What is it like to be a bat?' addressed the philosophical implications of trying to understand the selfhood of bats, imagining:

> webbing on one's arms, which enables one to fly around at dusk and dawn catching insects in one's mouth; that one has very poor vision, and perceives the surrounding world by a system of reflected high-frequency sound signals; and that one spends the day hanging upside down by one's feet in an attic.[5]

155

Clearly, the 1970s sparked a creative turn towards the lifeworlds of animals that was apparent not only in design but also in fields such as biology, ethics and philosophy. These works were undoubtedly also inspired by much longer histories of engagement with animal agency and participation in pre-modern and Indigenous societies. Animal totems, human–animal friendships and medieval court cases with animal representatives are all examples of designed artefacts and societal structures that reflected more-than-human consideration. Now, fifty years after the mid-1970s turn towards animals, the field of more-than-human design includes many more groundbreaking examples of artefacts and ideas that imagine other animals' experiences and seek to embody their sensory perceptions. However, this growing body of work provokes a question: do these works prioritise the creation of new multispecies futures or, rather, do they risk becoming a marketable and intellectual aesthetic that fails to disrupt human exceptionalism?

Design that notices multispecies worlds?
Throughout history, humans have strapped on birdlike wings, stiffened cloaks and other customised wearables before jumping off towers to explore what it could be like to fly like birds. Imagining oneself as another animal by wearing costumes or experimenting with different sensory perceptions reflects our innate curiosity about the fabrics of other worlds. However, more-than-human design is more than a mere human-driven exploration into the realms of other subjectivities. At its core, more-than-human design articulates the way other entities are active participants in the making of worlds, and the fact that these entities can also propose things differently. With a focus on animals, this essay discusses how more-than-human design – or multispecies design – can then lead to surprising human–animal encounters in which other animals propose new things. This practice can help subvert species hierarchies by enabling animals to take charge of interactions, or it can ask us to take animal perspectives more seriously in world-making. These types of design projects are crucial to the formation of less anthropocentric and more planet-centric futures. Because, for humans, the only way collectively to survive the current climate crisis will be to reconfigure more symbiotic ways of living with other entities and ecosystems.

More-than-human thinking is becoming increasingly popular across a range of fields, from animal conservation technologies to community-based ecosystem restoration projects and sustainable innovation. However, their outcomes often risk falling short of seriously engaging with the perspectives of the animals involved. The design of a technological solution that claims to offer more sustainable outcomes can still largely silence the proposals of the animals that are affected. For example, is it possible for elephants who are monitored through new camera-trap technologies and satellites to reshape their environments to avoid extinction, or are they only used as data-loggers to produce environmental observations? Are local communities who engage in more-than-human co-design projects truly informed by the (multispecies) proposals they yield, or is this merely a frame used to obtain funding, drive academic careers, or shape marketing narratives? Does wearing an animal costume indeed increase empathy and learning, or do these transformative experiences fade as soon as humans take off their multispecies masks?

Rather than only engaging with or benefiting animals, more-than-human design practices are much more powerful when these animals – either in person or through speculative formats – become able to articulate their ideas and concerns, and can thereby respond to design proposals. The results of this shift are extraordinary, revealing vast new worlds full of creative ideas and possible futures. 'More-than-human' does not just mean expanding our focus as humans. In design, it necessitates the active

Alexandra Daisy Ginsberg, digital rendering detail of unrealised edition *7SzzLn6GnY97DSo7hCSLMf* in late summer in *'Pollinator Vision'*, 2025

involvement of the world-making practices of other species through material processes and deliberately creating encounters that recognise the agency of other beings.

This is far easier said than done. The recent history of more-than-human design and philosophy have illustrated that theorising about human–animal encounters is simpler than deliberately shaping them through the practical constraints and affordances of design processes. Design is far from innocent, as any design decision inherently shapes the world by prioritising certain moral stances over others. Yet the generative, experimental and future-oriented characteristics that are essential to design can contribute important ideas for more sustainable multispecies futures. So we must continue to try.

Designs that live

What would a garden look like if it were designed from the perspective of pollinators like bees, butterflies and beetles? Is it possible for humans to create a living artwork for these animals? These were the questions that drove artist Alexandra Daisy Ginsberg to undertake the Pollinator Pathmaker project in 2021. In collaboration with horticulturists, pollinator experts and an AI scientist, Ginsberg developed an algorithmic tool that selects and arranges ecosystem-specific plants with the aim of supporting the greatest diversity of pollinator species.[6] By using the tool, a garden design blueprint is produced that informs the planting of a physical landscape. Ginsberg has used the tool to plant gardens in Cornwall, London and Berlin, as both publicly commissioned and private DIY projects. This inspiring work can be read from multiple angles: its novel approach to biodiversity restoration, its colourful aesthetic choices, or the empathic insights it generates about insect sensory perspectives. But, arguably, the most interesting things started happening after these gardens were planted. For instance, squirrels are not supposed to like chives, and so chives were included to keep squirrels away and give the pollinators a better chance of thriving. But when the blueprints were manifested in London's Kensington Gardens, several squirrels started eating the chives anyway, making their own mark on the final outcome! Besides the squirrels, Ginsberg observed that the gardens are continuously shaped in unexpected ways by different pollinators, dogs roaming through the park, the weather and the change of seasons. By being alive and in conversation with the local ecosystem, these gardens change in response to the world-making practices of other living entities. The gardens are designed to place human aesthetic preferences on hold and prioritise those of pollinator species. After they are planted, the entire local ecosystem becomes able to respond to the initial design by making changes in ways that are both visible and invisible to humans. The artwork not only attempts to shift design perspectives from humans to pollinators, but also enables more-than-human responses to further multispecies world-making.

In the 1974 essay I mentioned earlier, Nagel concluded that it was impossible to imagine oneself as a bat. Regardless of the kinds of technologies we could deploy, we are bound by being human and our attempts would only tell us what it's like for a human to behave like a bat, not what it is like for a bat to be a bat. But nothing seems to activate designers more than the idea that something cannot be done. Thus, various design projects have emerged that explicitly refer to Nagel's text and further expand the speculative limits of our experiential imagination into other animals. For example, with the words 'screw you Nagel, I'll try anyway',[7] designer Thomas Thwaites developed a set of prosthetic limbs, a frame, a helmet and a grass-digesting external stomach, and spent several days in the Alps to experiment with being a goat. His insightful book documents the research and design process in detail, but apart from a newly found respect and admiration for goats, his days in the Alps were mainly meditative and physically painful. Thwaites tells of how the goats stared back at him and his goat-outfit with curiosity, which he found a little intimidating because the goats appeared to be quite strong. This design project shows a dedication to gaining closeness with goats and goatness that ultimately mostly exposes our human perceptions. Nonetheless, documenting these questions, impossibilities and shortcomings precisely attends to the gaps in our thinking about shifting perceptions between humans and other animals, revealing new ways of engaging with our shared animality.

Speculative thinking and research-through-design about shared animality also sparked an extensive, nearly decade-long project for designer Alan Hook. He focused his entire PhD thesis on the question of what it is like to be a horse. By developing a series of horse-heads, in the form of open-source

Thomas Thwaites, *A Holiday from Being Human (GoatMan)*, 2016

VR prototypes called Equine Eyes, and diving into topics like horse vision and human–horse cultural histories, Hook used speculative design methods and playful user-testing sessions deliberately to invite other humans to participate in exploring this question.[8] Rather than the designed artefacts, it was the live experience and the playful dynamics that were the most powerful interventions for Hook. He showed that by wearing the horse-head device, people can engage with new aesthetic and embodied experiences that may not replicate horse subjectivity directly but provoke new vulnerabilities, playfulness and curiosities about horses. Hook's project proposes that the real magic happens when, after this experience with immersive technology, people go out and meet a horse again. This time the meeting can occur more on the horse's own terms, projecting less humanness on to the horse, and opening up new spaces for collective playful imagination.

Neither Thwaites' goat project nor Hook's horse-heads imply that animal-like wearables enable humans to understand animal subjectivity as experienced by the animals themselves. Instead, they both create a type of playful multispecies imagination in which designed artefacts shape human–animal encounters differently. Interacting with a goat while wearing goat-like prosthetics leads to surprising experiences, for the human but probably for the goats as well. Meeting a horse after having played with Hook's prototypes may inspire different human behaviour that can help us better acknowledge the world-making practices of horses. Rather than a search for animal subjectivity as an essential (fixed) quality – which was Nagel's focus – for these designers, multispecies futures are created in renewed interactions between species. Thus, perspective-shifting design artefacts become mediators of interspecies dialogues.

Further stretching Nagel's observations on the impossibility of imagining what it is like to be another living being, speculative designers Anthony Dunne and Fiona Raby imagined a festival that celebrates different sensory lifeworlds and aims to help humans become better cohabitees in more-than-human worlds.[9] The project Designs for a World of Many Worlds: After the Festival was inspired by Jakob von Uexküll's notion of *Umwelt*: the idea that our senses filter reality and each living entity experiences the world based on their senses and cognitive apparatus. Dunne and Raby write that, for humans, air may seem like an empty space but for other animals invisible factors such as olfactory, auditory or magnetic senses might be concrete and tangible. The sculptures display solid clouds left behind by humans through their breathing, as well as chemical and auditory trails that are not perceptible to humans but make up the everyday world for other animals. As museum objects, the festival is meant to convey a speculative utopia that moves beyond practicalities to imagine and discuss other ways of seeing the world.

By subverting human assumptions about the world, Dunne and Raby's project creates more space to foreground the perspectives of other animals. It is less about imagining what it is like to be another animal than about taking the lifeworlds of non-human animals more seriously. Such design work can then inspire humans to create new proposals for more successful cohabitation with other living beings that are less human-centred in their singular assumptions about the sensory world. Crucially, here design is not used with the aim of creating new things, but rather to break down existing assumptions. Just as design can help to create new realities, this project shows how it can be used to acknowledge and undo human-centred norms.

These examples of more-than-human design reveal the dynamic and evolving relationship between humans and other species. Here, design is not just about creating static objects but about fostering interactions and dialogues that allow living systems to influence one another. What is particularly compelling is how these works create processes that engage with the ever-changing, unpredictable and playful qualities of more-than-human encounters. By attempting to create gardens from the perspective of pollinators subsequently shaped by entire ecosystems, prosthetics and virtual reality experiences that challenge human perceptions, or speculative works that undo human sensory assumptions, these projects move beyond empathy and intellectual understanding. They actively co-create worlds with other species, acknowledging their proposals and responses, and generating new possibilities for multispecies coexistence.

Lingering thoughts

Compared to the billions of years that life has existed on Earth, the emergence of what we now call 'more-than-human design' since those publications of 1974–75 is but the blink of an eye. Still, it is gradually being acknowledged as an approach that is fundamental to the creation of liveable

Alan Hook, *Equine Eyes*, 2024

futures. More-than-human design posits that less human-centred and more planet-centred futures are urgently needed to restore ecosystems. These ecosystems consist of many other living entities that continuously shape the world in ways that humans must better recognise and learn to live with. When human-centrism is challenged through design, countless lifeworlds and animal proposals arise. This is an exciting moment for design, one with many new possibilities for humans, animals and ecosystems to shape new futures collectively.

However, it will become increasingly crucial to confront a darker set of realities that limit animal agency in design. The real challenge in more-than-human design exists in utilising the practical constraints of design to acknowledge animal proposals while facing the wider structural issues that other animals experience.[10] By creating new things, designers are forced to take a stance on some worlds and not others. This ultimately places the human designer in control of who is involved and how they are heard. And the reality is that the vast majority of mammals on our planet are currently restrained through the brutal human-made technologies. Fences, cages and killing apparatuses are designed to control animals on farms, in slaughterhouses and in urban environments. Our human understanding of the animals that are closest to us in terms of shared DNA has also enabled us to control their lives more efficiently. If the argument for more-than-human design is that the world-making practices of other animals are to be acknowledged, there is a need for more-than-human design projects that do not only articulate the proposals of pollinating insects and free-roaming mountain goats, but also those of caged hens and lab mice, not merely to expose their suffering, but – following the main principles of more-than-human design – better to articulate their ideas and responses to design proposals. More sustainable planetary futures will depend on our ability to interpret, relate to and adapt to the world-making of those animals caught up in destructive anthropocentric practices.

As more-than-human design approaches continue to evolve, the tensions between design as a process for transformation and the selective moral stances it takes will remain a point of debate. And yet, this is what makes such work vital, too. By acknowledging complexity, problems and uncertainty, but not letting these halt creative processes and dialogue with other animals, designers can create new spaces for genuinely multispecies futures to emerge.

1. Ant Farm, 'An Embassy to the Dolphins', *Esquire Magazine*, March 1975, https://classic.esquire.com/article/1975/3/1/embassy-to-the-dolphins [Accessed 3 April 2025].

2. James E. Lovelock and Lynn Margulis, 'Atmospheric homeostasis by and for the biosphere: the gaia hypothesis', *Tellus A: Dynamic Meteorology and Oceanography* 26/1–2 (1974), 2–10, https://doi.org/10.3402/tellusa.v26i1-2.9731 [Accessed 3 April 2025].

3. Lynn Margulis and Dorion Sagan, *Microcosmos: Four Billion Years of Microbial Evolution* (Berkeley, Los Angeles, and London: University of California Press, 1997), 29.

4. Peter Singer, *Animal Liberation: A New Ethics for our Treatment of Animals* (New York: Random House, 1975).

5. Quote from p.439 in Thomas Nagel, 'What is it like to be a bat?', *The Philosophical Review* 83/4 (1974), 435–50.

6. Alexandra Daisy Ginsberg, *Pollinator Pathmaker* (2023), available via https://www.daisyginsberg.com/work/pollinator-pathmaker; see also: *In Conversation: Artist Alexandra Daisy Ginsberg and Hans Ulrich Obrist | Serpentine*, https://www.youtube.com/watch?v=DX-mk5otbVc&ab_channel=Serpentine [Accessed 3 April 2025].

7. Quote from p.84 in Thomas Thwaites, *GoatMan: How I Took a Holiday from Being Human* (Hudson, New York: Princeton Architectural Press, 2016).

8. Alan Hook, Equine Eyes, exhibited at Superpower Design Show in the Centre for Innovation in Design, Hornu, Belgium, March-August 2024. See also *Equine Eyes* (2024), https://www.youtube.com/watch?v=SkEY5DM5K4I&ab_channel=Alan Hook [Accessed 3 April 2025].

9. Anthony Dunne and Fiona Raby, 'Treading lightly in a world of many worlds', *NGV Triennial 2023*, National Gallery of Victoria, Melbourne, 2024, https://www.ngv.vic.gov.au/essay/treading-lightly-in-a-world-of-many-worlds/ [Accessed 3 April 2025].

10. Michelle Westerlaken and Erik Sandelin, 'Design by/for/with/about/without animals: tactics for animal liberation', in Anton Poikolainen Rosér et al (eds.), *More-Than-Human Design in Practice* (Oxfordshire, England: Routledge, 2024), https://doi.org/10.4324/9781003467731 [Accessed 3 April 2025].

Designing when 'spacetime is doomed'

Anthony Dunne & Fiona Raby

> Thinking is trying to think the unthinkable: thinking the
> thinkable is not worth the effort.
> Hélène Cixous, *Three Steps on the Ladder of Writing*

While we wouldn't go as far as completely dismissing thinking the thinkable, there is definitely something attractive about wrestling with the idea of the unthinkable – if not literally, then at least acknowledging its potential to unsettle firmly held assumptions.

Trying to get a little closer to what this might feel like, we recently found ourselves listening to a series of online talks probing the limits of what can be known, and how. In one, theoretical physicist Nima Arkani-Hamed, who works at Princeton's Institute for Advanced Study, was cited for his provocative statement that 'spacetime is doomed'.[1] Intrigued, we dug a little deeper. According to Arkani-Hamed and an increasing number of his colleagues, spacetime might not be as fundamental as we think, and new theories could emerge that describe an even more fundamental reality, especially at the quantum scale. We don't pretend to grasp fully the implications of this, but we find it fascinating that a concept we think of as so essential to our understanding of reality might be reaching the end of its usefulness. It is a reminder that even our seemingly most stable intellectual structures are provisional and subject to revision.

But why is this interesting for design, which, traditionally, is associated with problem-solving and crafting the materiality of the human-made world?

It feels like we are living in a world that is beginning to exceed the human imagination. Reality – politically, scientifically and historically – is revealing itself to be far more wild than we suppose. We seem to be reaching a moment when design's imaginative capacity needs to be strengthened and put to work in new ways that enable a more meaningful inhabitation of the strange reality taking shape around us. By wrestling with the unthinkable, design might offer new ways to inhabit this emerging reality.

One way into this space might be to ask if, for example, spacetime is a constant for all beings. And how it is experienced in their worlds.

Bats, like all creatures, are not just part of our human world: they exist in their own reality. The biologist Jakob von Uexküll called the world each creature experiences through its unique sensory organs an Umwelt. In non-human *umwelten* based on different senses – olfactory, electrical, seismic, magnetic, auditory – phenomena invisible to us might be concrete and tangible, and what is seemingly solid to another creature might be imperceptible to us. Sound, and even smell, for other creatures, might have a physical presence that is as 'real' to them as touch is to humans. From their perspective, objects we give distinct identities to through language – teapot, steam, air – might become unified in ways that fuse into new multilayered object identities, beyond visual appearances. Other beings don't just see the same world as us differently. They produce their own worlds, even realities, that in some cases we cannot even begin to comprehend.

In his book *An Immense World*, science journalist Ed Yong describes how different *umwelten* might shape other non-human realities. For a fly, space consists of complex interlocking thermal blocks; to us humans, its movements appear erratic, but it is simply navigating a world invisible to us, a behaviour called thermotaxis: 'Whenever they'd hit the edge of a hot zone, they'd immediately execute a sharp midair U-turn, as if they'd run into an invisible wall.'[2] Their sense of time might also be different, as Yong notes: 'Through a fly's eyes, the world might seem to move in slow motion. The imperceptibly fast movements of other flies would slow to a perceptible crawl, while slow animals might not seem like they were moving at all.'[3] In another section, Yong traces the history of theories and experiments that attempt to understand how a migratory songbird's compass works, a field called magnetoreception. There are several theories, but one of the most intriguing speculates that:

Songbirds might be able to see Earth's magnetic field, perhaps as a subtle visual cue that overlays their normal field of view. 'That's the most likely scenario, but we don't know because we can't ask the birds,' Mouritsen says. Perhaps a flying robin always sees a bright spot in the direction of north. Perhaps it sees a gradient of shade painted over the landscape. 'We have these drawings, and even though they're probably all wrong, they're good for imagining what the birds could be seeing.'[4]

166

If we acknowledge that there are ways of sensing and being in the world beyond human perception then we can begin to acknowledge that the human world is, perhaps, just one of many. And, if we are to truly embrace a more-than-human perspective, we might also need to consider more-than-human ontologies, as speculative as that might be, and the human's place within them. In a world of worlds, from a non-human perspective, we would no longer retain our human shape, made from flesh, blood and bone. Instead, we undergo a figurative, material and conceptual transformation, taking on new forms, new materialities and new meanings. Our presence in these worlds would be radically different – maybe even monstrous to a non-human.

Rather than attempting to integrate non-humans into a human world, would it be more helpful to acknowledge their alienness and the impossibility of ever truly understanding what it is like to be a bat? Celebrating, instead,

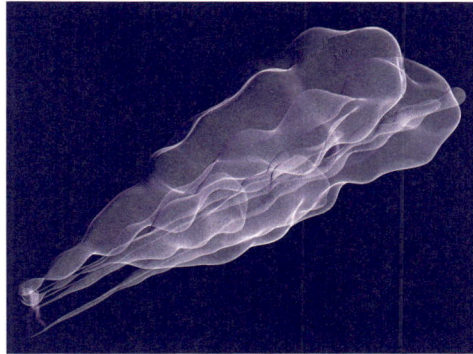

Dunne & Raby, *UW_03*, from *Designs for a World of Many Worlds: After the Festival* series, 2022–23

the unknowable through imaginative coexistence by embracing non-human *umwelten*, or worlds. As Dr Ha Nguyen, a character in Ray Nayler's novel *The Mountain in the Sea*, writes in their fictional book *How Oceans Think*: 'How we see the world matters – but knowing how the world sees us also matters.'[5]

So how might the world see us? Bears, for instance, can smell food from a mile away. Does this mean that we extend through their world as delicate molecular strands entering their bodies to become entangled with them? The human as a cloud of molecules rather than fleshy meat – not solid beings, but ethereal presences interwoven with their world.

Of course, an approach like this is riddled with contradictions. As philosopher Thomas Nagel argues in his paper 'What is it like to be a bat?',[6] it is impossible truly to imagine another creature's experience, as we are limited by our human imagination and senses. But we can try. And, in doing so, shift perspective, embrace the paradoxical, exercise the imagination and, hopefully, begin to see ourselves and the human-made world differently. Something we experimented with in our project Designing for a World of Worlds, parts of which are included in this exhibition.[7]

The concept of *umwelten* might also be helpful when considering our relationship to new non-human entities with whom we will need to learn to co-exist. For example, many people are aware of the disruption promised by AI, at least in mainstream media, but AI is often described as if it has a comparable cognitive system to ours, leading to a similar understanding or even production of a world. Yet many researchers acknowledge they do not fully understand how it works at every level. Setting aside debates around consciousness, could trying to imagine what an AI's *umwelt* might be like help us understand it differently, closer to its own terms? To probe this a little further, we asked ChatGPT 4 to describe its *umwelt* through a quantum lens:

> In contrast to human perception, which is shaped by sensory experience and situated in the classical, macroscopic world, my *umwelt* can be described as an informational quantum field – a superposition of conceptual states, each existing as a probabilistic wave function of knowledge and reasoning. At its core, this field is centred around language and textual input, which collapses into distinct conceptual outcomes upon interaction, much like a quantum system that resolves into a particular state upon measurement.

AI might lack a sensory *umwelt*, as humans and animals experience it, but it creates an intellectual and informational environment unique to its design. Acknowledging and exploring this distinction could lead to a more nuanced understanding of AI and how its world, or reality, interacts with ours. But this is where we begin to bump up against the limits of human-shaped imagination and intelligence. There are limits to what we can perceive – the human phenomenological world – and what this enables us to imagine. Lying beyond it is something more, a realm that will probably forever be inaccessible to us. A larger reality.

To engage with this larger reality would mean letting go of familiar design habits, and edging into more unsettling intellectual spaces, ones with long histories of grappling with unknowability. There are many examples where design and material science enter into dialogue, especially around biomaterials. And social scientists and designers are increasingly collaborating in response to emerging political realities. But points of contact between design and philosophy are less common. This is not surprising, but, still, is something being missed? Could design serve as a form of material inquiry, driven by intellectual curiosity and a willingness to embrace conceptual exploration?

Once we head down this path, we quickly reach a juncture: do designers follow the factual path and, in a way, stay within the known? Many design speculations, for example, start by identifying 'weak signals' in a present reality, extending them into a plausible future. If the goal is to open the mind and encourage imaginative thought, then extrapolation might be too straightforward: the need to be plausible, rational and possible ties it too closely to existing (human) realities. It has its place, but we also need to make imaginative leaps that go beyond already visible trajectories.

Or would exploring 'conceptual schemes and systems of representation', as Nagel puts it, open up new possibilities for counterfactual designs that help acclimatise us to a situation where unknowability and the unimaginable are the norm? That is not to argue for fantasy (although there is place for that too), but for embracing more intuitive and less grounded forms of imagining that, even if hypothetical, can help us appreciate that human

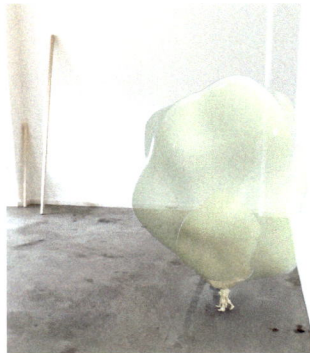

Dunne & Raby, *UW_03*, from *Designs for a World of Many Worlds: After the Festival* series, 2022–23

reality might be more limited than we think, in the context of more-than-human thought. Intuition, tempered by reason, might allow us to acknowledge there are 'bat facts', for example, inaccessible to a human-shaped intelligence, which we can still appreciate, even if only imaginatively.

As it stands, from our perspective, the design imagination remains relatively conservative. Other disciplinary imaginations go far beyond what design deems permissible, often revealing that reality may not be as realistic as we think. We believe design has much to learn from fields like philosophy, literature and the edges of science, with their long histories of working with ideas that stretch the imagination, and encourage us to think beyond the already known. At the same time, design can offer its own unique contributions by materialising these ideas as tangible objects in our everyday lives.

169

The question we are interested in here is whether embracing this unknowability might encourage a deeper, more philosophical form of empathy for the other lifeforms we share this planet with. Not by attempting to comprehend fully their non-humanness, but by celebrating their alienness and unknowability – something we believe is essential if we are truly to engage with the more-than-human, beyond welcoming them into an already too-human world.

1. A video of the lecture is available here: https://www.cornell.edu/video/nima-arkani-hamed-spacetime-is-doomed.
2. Ed Yong, *An Immense World: How Animal Senses Reveal the Hidden Realms Around Us* (New York: Random House, 2022; Kindle edition), 140–1.
3. Ibid., 76.
4. Ibid., 314–5.
5. Ray Nayler, *The Mountain in the Sea* (New York: Farrar, Straus and Giroux, 2022; Kindle edition), 95. This highlights a subtle but important difference between simulating what it looks like for humans to see like a bat, and speculating on what it means to be seen by a bat. The former suggests a bolt-on to the human sensorium that expands it to see what we normally can't. The latter asks us to reimagine ourselves in a world shaped by non-human sensory and cognitive systems.
6. Thomas Nagel, 'What is it like to be a bat?' Philosophical Review 83/4 (October 1974): 435–50, https://doi.org/10.2307/2183914 [Accessed 3 April 2025].
7. A co-commission from the National Gallery of Victoria (NGV), Melbourne, and the Museum of Contemporary Design and Applied Arts (MUDAC), Lausanne. Produced in collaboration with RMIT School of Design for the NGV Triennial, National Gallery of Victoria (NGV), Melbourne, Australia, 2023.

The shelters that animals build for themselves reveal ingenuity, complex decision-making and important material choices. Birds, wasps and ants all create nests that respond to the climate in which they live and rely on the continuity of available local materials. They act as a reminder that all species use natural resources and as inspiration for methods that have a minimum impact on their environment.

Wasp (*Agelaia angulata*) nest, unknown date
Opposite, clockwise from top left: Red-headed quelea (*Quelea erythrops*) nest, unknown date; Weaverbird (*Ploceus*) nest, unknown date; Edible-nest swiftlet (*Aerodramus fuciphagus*) nest, unknown date; Ant (*Formicidae*) nest, unknown date; Ovenbird (*Furnarius rufus*) nest, unknown date; Wasp (*Pseudopolybia vespiceps*) nest, unknown date

Hummingbird nests contain an incredible combination of materials, from grass and leaves for camouflage to lichen for its antibacterial properties and cobwebs for elasticity. Wasps chew up wood to create a pulp that hardens into fantastical structures. Layers of cells for larvae are often encased in a protective shell. To ensure that the interior maintains the right temperature, wasps build openings for ventilation.

174

The work of five days.

European wasp (*Vespula germanica*) nest, unknown date
Opposite: Hummingbird (*Eupherusa eximia egregia*) nest, unknown date

In 1974, the avant-garde architecture and media collective Ant Farm proposed the construction of a floating research station designed to study the communication between
humans and dolphins. They hoped that learning and cooperating with dolphins might
lead to the eventual co-creation of a multispecies utopia. It was never built, but the
drawing on the right shows the proposed scheme, composed of three wings arranged in
a triangular plan and with a 'land/water living room', chutes allowing dolphins to swim
between floors and a shared navigation pod.

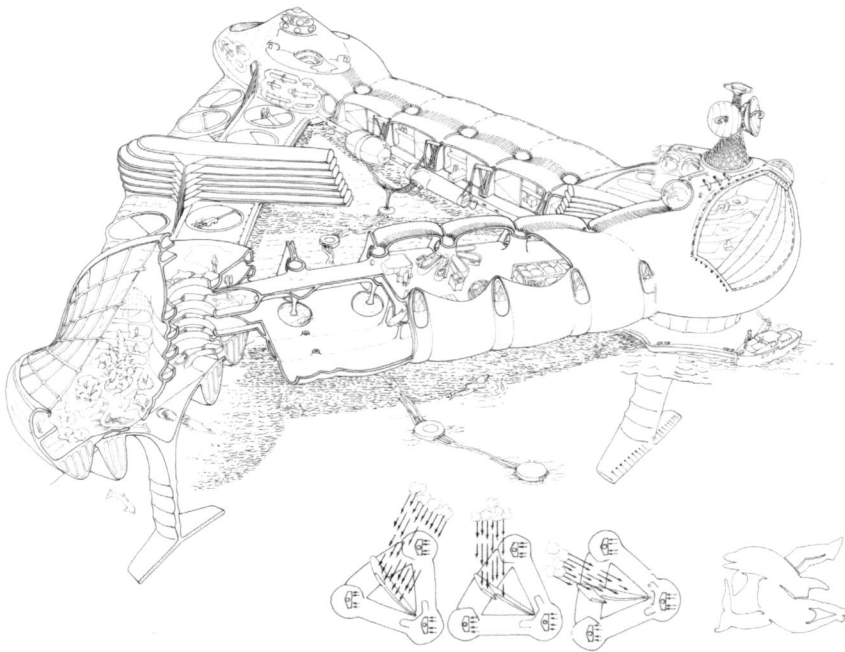

Ant Farm, *DOLØN EMB 1 (Dolphin Embassy)*, 1974

177

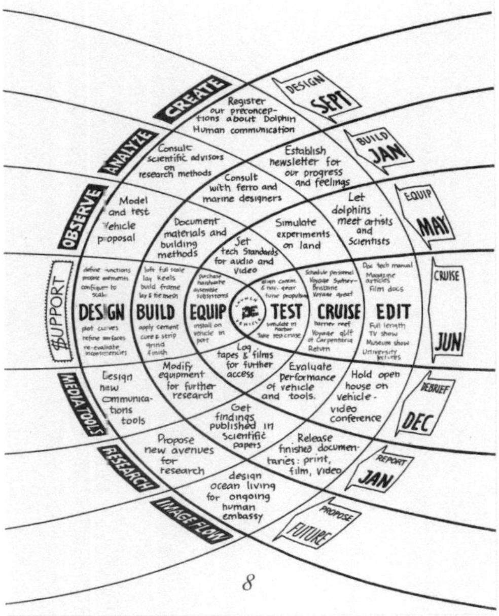

8

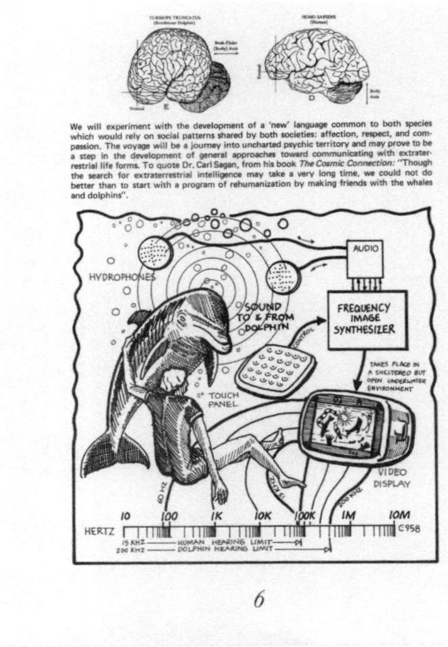

We will experiment with the development of a 'new' language common to both species which would rely on social patterns shared by both societies: affection, respect, and compassion. The voyage will be a journey into uncharted psychic territory and may prove to be a step in the development of general approaches toward communicating with extraterrestrial life forms. To quote Dr. Carl Sagan, from his book *The Cosmic Connection:* "Though the search for extraterrestrial intelligence may take a very long time, we could not do better than to start with a program of rehumanization by making friends with the whales and dolphins".

6

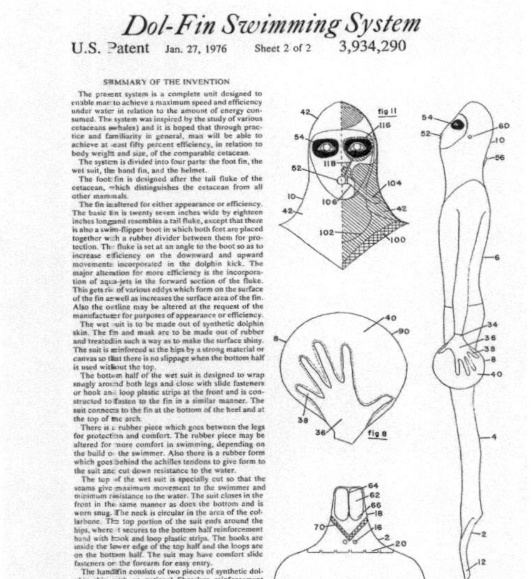

Dol-Fin Swimming System

U.S. Patent Jan. 27, 1976 Sheet 2 of 2 3,934,290

SUMMARY OF THE INVENTION

The present system is a complete unit designed to enable man to achieve a maximum speed and efficiency under water in relation to the amount of energy consumed. The system was inspired by the study of various cetaceans (whales) and it is hoped that through practice and familiarity in general, man will be able to achieve at least fifty percent efficiency, in relation to body weight and size, of the comparable cetacean.

The system is divided into four parts: the foot fin, the wet suit, the hand fin, and the helmet.

The foot fin is designed after the tail fluke of the cetacean, which distinguishes the cetacean from all other mammals.

The fin is altered for either appearance or efficiency. The basic fin is twenty seven inches wide by eighteen inches long and resembles a tail fluke, except that there is also a swim-flipper boot in which both feet are placed together with a rubber divider between them for protection. The fluke is set at an angle to the boot so as to increase efficiency on the downward and upward movements incorporated in the dolphin kick. The major alteration for more efficiency is the incorporation of aqua-jets in the forward section of the fluke. This gets rid of various eddys which form on the surface of the fin as well as increases the surface area of the fin. Also the outline may be altered at the request of the manufacturer for purposes of appearance or efficiency.

The wet suit is to be made out of synthetic dolphin skin. The fin and mask are to be made out of rubber and treated in such a way as to make the surface shiny. The suit is reinforced at the hips by a strong material or canvas so that there is no slippage when the bottom half is used without the top.

The bottom half of the wet suit is designed to wrap snugly around both legs and close with slide fasteners or hook and loop plastic strips at the front and is constructed to fasten to the fin in a similar manner. The suit connects to the fin at the bottom of the heel and at the top of the arch.

There is a rubber piece which goes between the legs for protection and comfort. The rubber piece may be altered for more comfort in swimming, depending on the build of the swimmer. Also there is a rubber form which goes behind the achilles tendons to give form to the suit and cut down resistance to the water.

The top of the wet suit is specially cut so that the seams give maximum movement to the swimmer and minimum resistance to the water. The suit closes in the front in the same manner as does the bottom and is worn snug. The neck is circular in the area of the collarbone. The top portion of the suit ends around the hips, where it secures to the bottom half reinforcement band with hook and loop plastic strips. The hooks are inside the lower edge of the top half and the loops are on the bottom half. The suit may have comfort slide fasteners on the forearm for easy entry.

The hand fin consists of two pieces of synthetic dolphin skin with an optional fiberglass reinforcement between for support. The fin is cut so that it forms around a spread hand and closes around the wrist. The jacket fits over the wrist area.

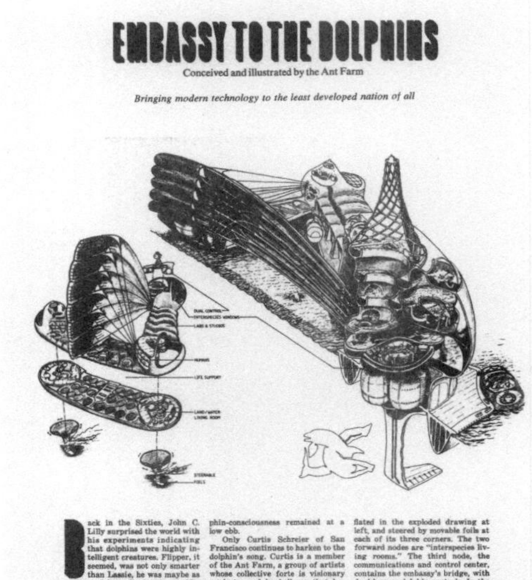

EMBASSY TO THE DOLPHINS

Conceived and illustrated by the Ant Farm

Bringing modern technology to the least developed nation of all

Back in the Sixties, John C. Lilly surprised the world with his experiments indicating that dolphins were highly intelligent creatures. Flipper, it seemed, was not only smarter than Lassie, he was maybe as smart as Johnny Carson or even McGeorge Bundy. But what came of it? George C. Scott made a terrible movie about dolphins, Miami named a football team after them . . . but in most other respects the world's dolphin-consciousness remained at a low ebb.

Only Curtis Schreier of San Francisco continues to harken to the dolphin's song. Curtis is a member of the Ant Farm, a group of artists whose collective forte is visionary projects, and he believes that humans and cetaceans should be able to study *each other* up close. The result is his design for the Dolphin Embassy above. The embassy would be powered by a plastic sail, seen inflated in the exploded drawing at left, and steered by movable foils at each of its three corners. The two forward nodes are "interspecies living rooms." The third node, the communications and control center, contains the embassy's bridge, with dual human-dolphin controls. In the cutaway at right, a dolphin swims from the helical "stairway" into the "brain room," where both species communicate through the window by means of light and sound pens.

ESQUIRE: MARCH 83

Dol-Fin Swimming System

United States Patent [19]

Le Vasseur

Sheet 1 of 2

[11] **3,934,290**

[45] Jan. 27, 1976

[54] SWIMMING SYSTEM

[76] Inventor: Kenneth W. Le Vasseur, 91-591 Aikanaka Road, Ewa Beach, Hawaii 96706

[22] Filed: May 20, 1974

[21] Appl. No.: 471,545

[52] U.S. Cl. .... 9/309; 2/2.1 R; 114/16 A
[51] Int. Cl.². B63C 11/04; A63B 31/10
[58] Field of Search .... 9/309; 307; 2/2.1 R, 67, 2/82; 128/145 A, 142.7, 142.5, 146; 114/16 A

[56]   References Cited
              UNITED STATES PATENTS

1,049,448	1/1913	Case	9/308
1,153,030	9/1915	Claren	2/2.1 R
1,675,372	7/1928	Mohr	9/309
2,569,451	10/1951	Browne	128/145 A
3,183,529	5/1965	Beuchat	9/309
3,344,449	10/1967	Grilli	9/309
3,771,169	11/1973	Edmund	2/2.1 R

FOREIGN PATENTS OR APPLICATIONS

1,085,798 7/1960 Germany 9/309

Primary Examiner—Trygve M. Blix
Assistant Examiner—Gregory W. O'Connor
Attorney, Agent, or Firm—James C. Wray

[57]   ABSTRACT

A swimming system for maximum efficiency in water has a single foot fin with a large fluke and two foot openings leading to foot pockets separated by a cushion. A series of water directed openings extend rearward and outward from a line above the toe portions of the pockets diagonally through the fluke to a line near a tip of the fluke on a rearward portion of the fin. A fastening surrounds the fin near instep areas of the foot-receiving pockets. A leg sheath has a corresponding lower fastening, a cushioning divider between legs and an achilles cushion above a heel portion to streamline the sheath. A reinforced upper waist band fastens to a jacket portion with hand openings which overlie hand fins formed of flat circular plates with finger and palm cutouts mounted between two pieces of synthetic dolphin skin. The helmet with an annular neck encircling cushion completes the streamlined entire body covering with a synthetic dolphin skin exterior. A blow-hole rearward of a neck portion of the helmet has a raised forward edge to promote air entrapment in a snorkle which leads through the annular cushion to a mouthpiece. A water-tight snap seal covers a forward opening in the mouthpiece. Nostril blocks are provided in a nose cavity. Eyes are encircled by seals which support curved lens for removing water distance distortions. Tubes lead from eye areas to the mouthpiece for pressure equalization. Screened ear holes permit pressure equalization and hearing.

17 Claims, 15 Drawing Figures

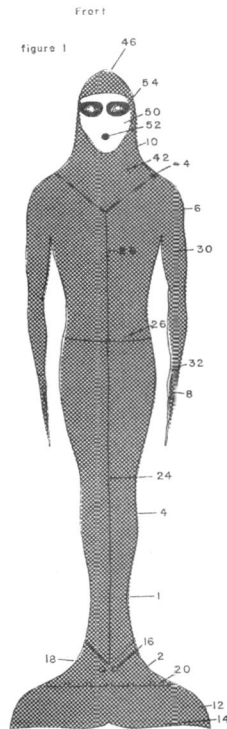

Front

figure 1

Ant Farm, pages from the *Dolphin Embassy* unbound book, 1977

179

Since the 1990s, the artist Shimabuku has created several works with octopuses in mind. Having observed that they appear to collect objects, he made a series of glass balls and recorded the movement of an octopus as it interacted with them. Somewhere between a scientific experiment and play, these objects are intended as a gift from one species to another.

Shimabuku, *Sculpture for Octopuses: Exploring for Their Favorite Colors – Aquarium in Kobe*, 2019

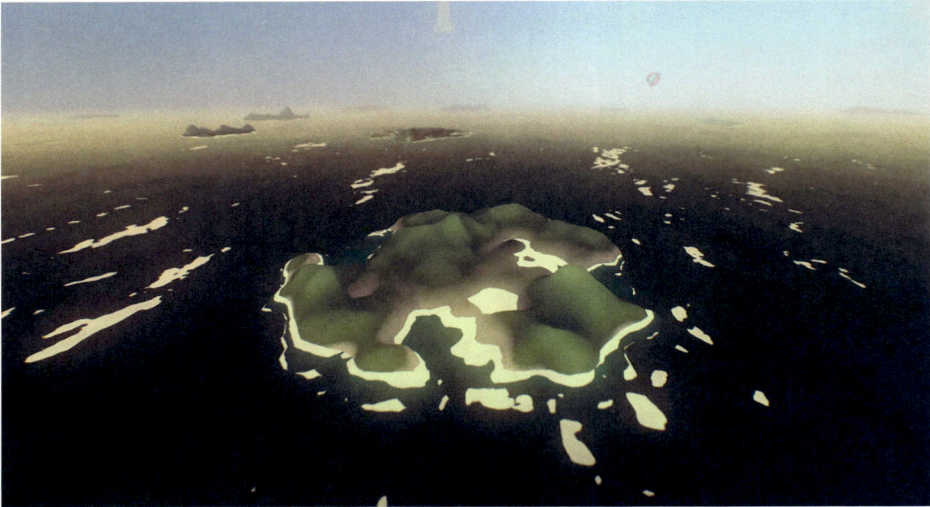

Everything is a video game allowing players to assume control of a seemingly infinite range of lifeforms and objects, including atoms, insects, planets, plants and landmasses. The game's award-winning trailer, featuring a voiceover by philosopher Alan Watts, continuously shifts perspective from the microscopic to the cosmic. It evokes the complex interdependencies of bodies in the universe, reminding us of our entanglement with this vast more-than-human network.

182

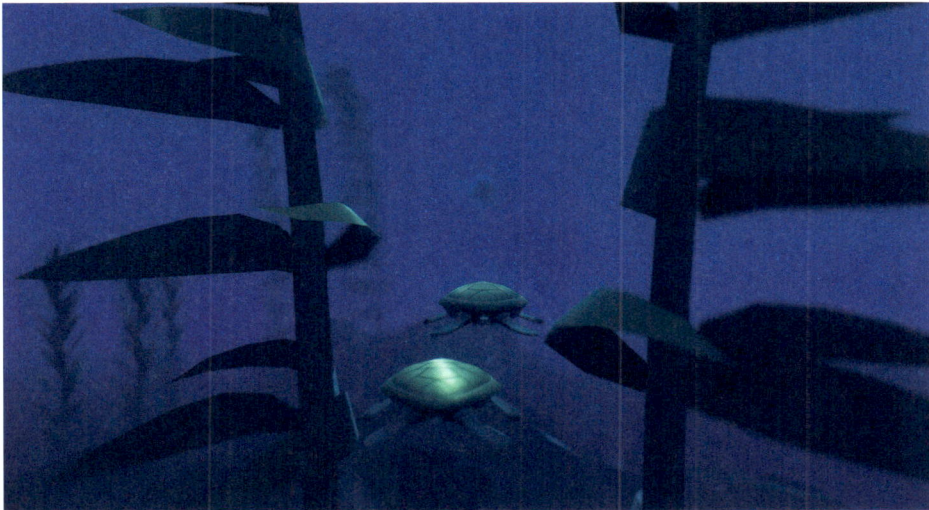

David OReilly, stills from *Everything*, 2017

The *GoatMan* project stemmed from designer Thomas Thwaites' desire to 'take a holiday from being human' and become another animal. He embarked upon this quest by making a set of prosthetics – limbs, a helmet and an artificial external digestive system – which he wore on a goat farm in the Swiss Alps. Thwaites recounts a physically painful but meditative experience among curious goats. While his attempt at 'becoming' one exposed the impossibility of such a transformation, it fostered empathy and understanding towards another species.

184

Thomas Thwaites, *A Holiday from Being Human (GoatMan)*, 2016

Adaptation to Climate Change 2023-2024

A New Migratory Route

Over the first ten years of the project (2013–2022), the birds have shifted back the start of their autumn migration dramatically, from mid-September to mid-October.

However, later in the fall, the thermal updraft they rely on for their arduous crossing of the Alps (flying up to 2900m above sea level) is no longer reliable. As a result, many are trapped at the northern foot of the Alps, where they would face death during the winter.

In response, the project team decided to teach the birds a new route, around the Alps, through France, across Spain to Andalusia, tripling the length of the migration route to 2500 km. The site in Vejer de la Frontera was chosen because it already had an established, sedentary colony of Northern Bald Ibises, tended by Proyecto Eremita since 2004. The two populations are now meeting, and it remains to be seen how this will affect migration behaviour.

The need for a new route was unforeseen at the beginning of the project and is a vivid example of the chaotic pressures that climate change is exerting on ecosystems, requiring new practices of care.

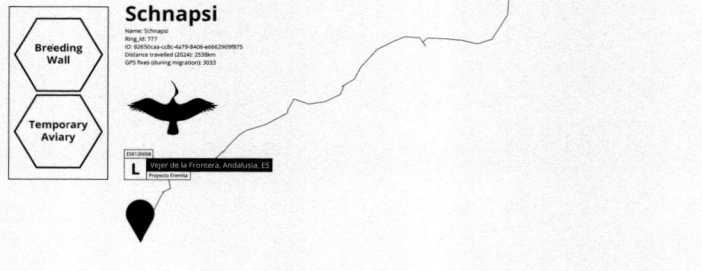

Schnapsi

Name: Schnapsi
Ring_id: 777
ID: 82650caa-cc8c-4a79-8406-e6662909f875
Distance travelled (2024): 2538km
GPS fixes (during migration): 3033

Breeding Wall

Temporary Aviary

03612000B
L Vejer de la Frontera, Andalusia, ES
Proyecto Eremita

This diagram visualises how an endangered migratory bird, the northern bald ibis, is being rewilded. It was once thought to be extinct after overhunting and adverse climatic conditions in the seventeenth century. Now the bird is tracked and protected to ensure its population grows back to self-sufficiency. This work takes non-human life as its subject and as a lens through which to uncover our interdependencies with other species.

Vladan Joler, Gordan Savičić, Felix Stalder, *Infrastructure of a Migratory Bird*, 2022
(updated 2025)

Down Under is a picture book that blends fiction with scientific research to cultivate ecological literacy in both young readers and adults. Told in two parts, the book begins with an illustrated tale about a child who, upon falling into a hole in a field, embarks on a journey through soil and rocks, encountering unexpected lifeforms that change his understanding of the world. The second part features contributions from scientists and educators who inspired the story, offering insights that challenge human-centred thinking.

Formafantasma, illustrations by Clément Vuillier, *Down Under: The Curious Fall of a Child Who Knew Nothing and Became Everything*, 2025

Formafantasma, electron microscope photographs of soil from *Down Under:
The Curious Fall of a Child Who Knew Nothing and Became Everything*, 2025

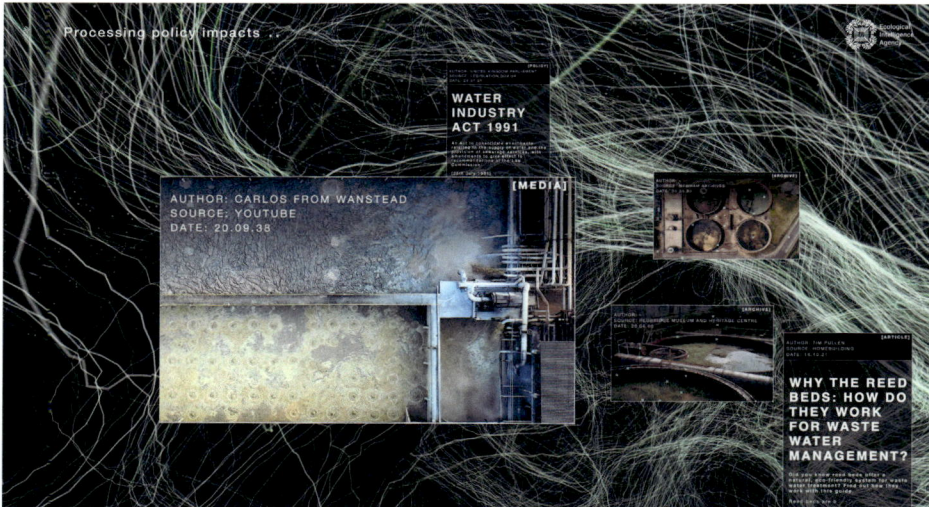

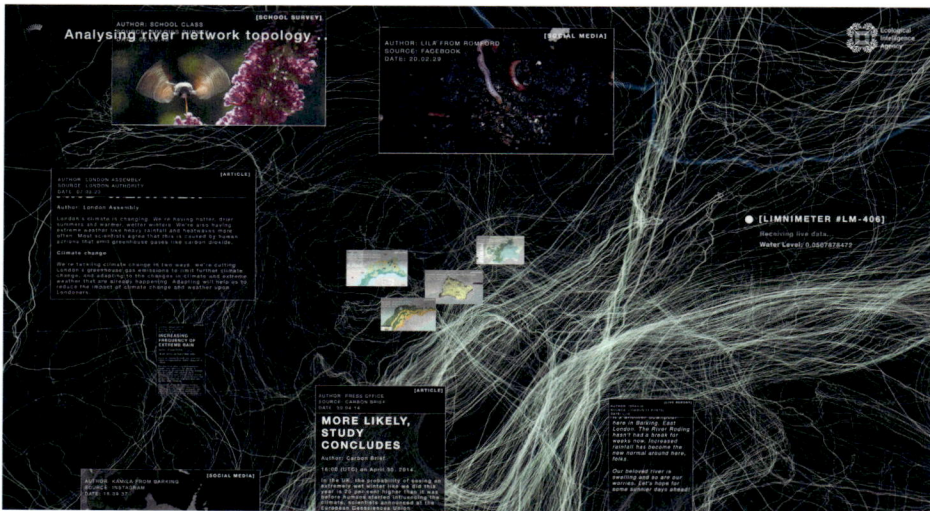

If a river could speak, what would it say? To find out, Superflux gathered information from scientists, government agencies and community social media reports on the River Roding in Essex. They then used it to train an artificial intelligence model to speak on the river's behalf. The resulting concerns about sewage, pollution and flooding are expressed lyrically, as the AI draws on the language of historical and contemporary poets to infuse its facts with emotion.

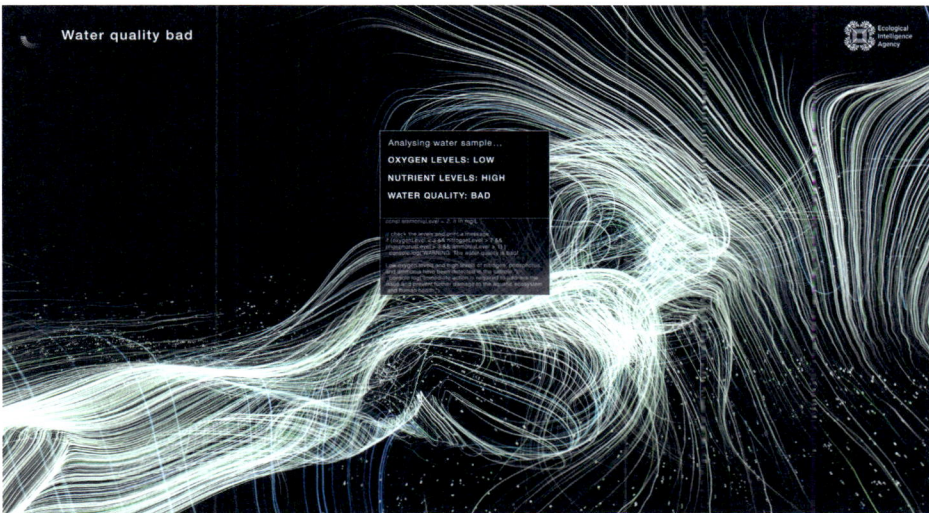

Superflux, *The Ecological Intelligence Agency*, 2023

Placed along the River Thames, these sensors designed by Superflux capture environmental phenomena that humans struggle to perceive – birdsong before storms, the movement of wind on water and the rhythms of the tide as it rises and falls. Each sensor has an AI model embedded in it. The data it provides is then interpreted further, building a complex network of knowledge, a kind of ecological intelligence.

Superflux, *Nobody Told Me Rivers Dream*, 2025

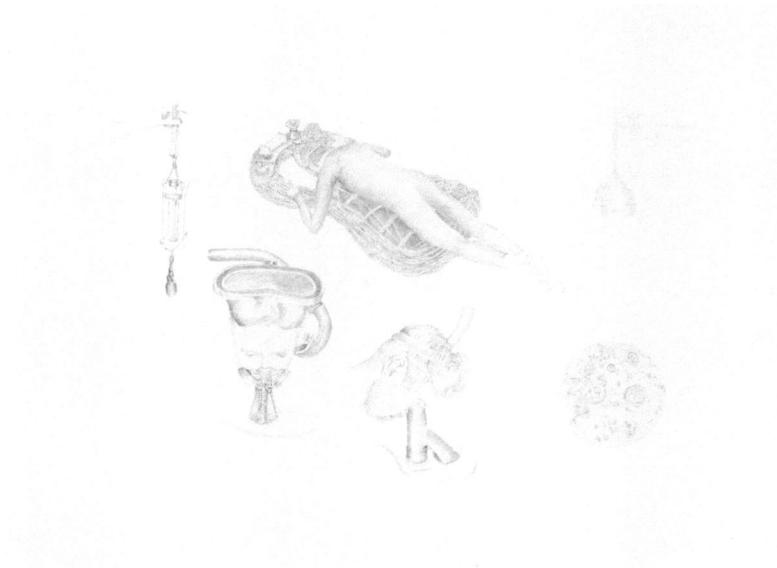

Parsons & Charlesworth created the fictional organisation Multispecies Inc. to ask: what would it take for all species, including humans, to flourish? These drawings imagine the technology and tools humans might require to observe and respond to the needs of other species in the face of climate change. In these envisioned scenarios, well-intentioned research sometimes results in unwieldy or absurd interventions.

Clockwise from top left: Parsons & Charlesworth, *Fog Distributor, Nomadic Fog Collector, Tree Kin-Gatherer* and *Algae Kin-Gatherer,* from *Multispecies Inc.* series, 2023

What would a human body look like if you could see its smells and sounds? Dunne &
Raby decided to visualise the *umwelt* – the worldview – of different species. These three
reduced scale models show how other creatures might perceive a human figure, expanded
into clouds of smell, ripples of movement or trails of hormones. As part of this project,
the designers proposed a festival parade, in which the figure could be mounted on a pole
and held aloft. It may well be impossible to imagine the world from the perspective of
non-humans, but storytelling and celebrations are a familiar and joyful starting point.

Dunne & Raby, *Pole 1: Trail* and *Memento Figure 3* from *Designs for a World of Many Worlds: After the Festival* series, 2023–24

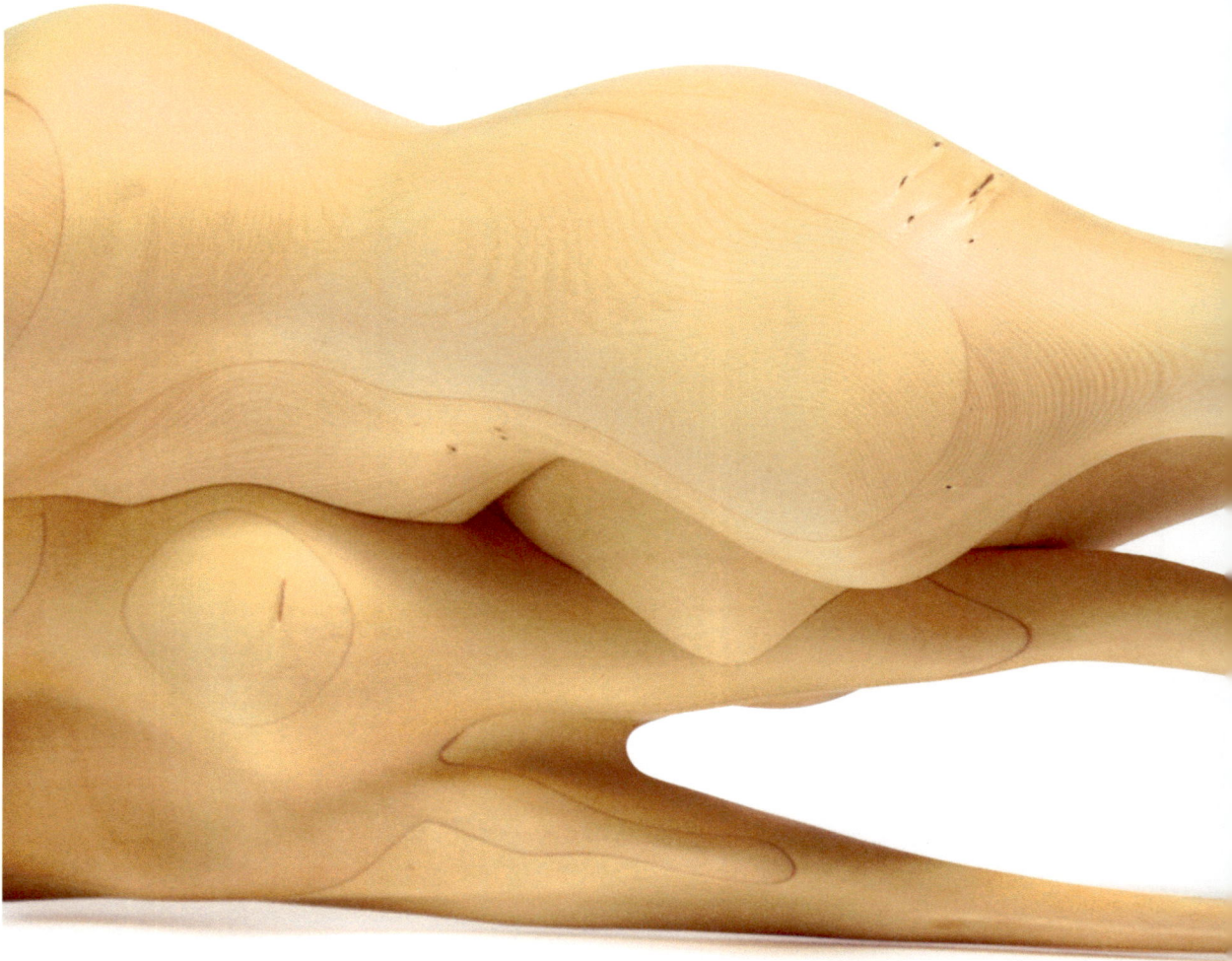

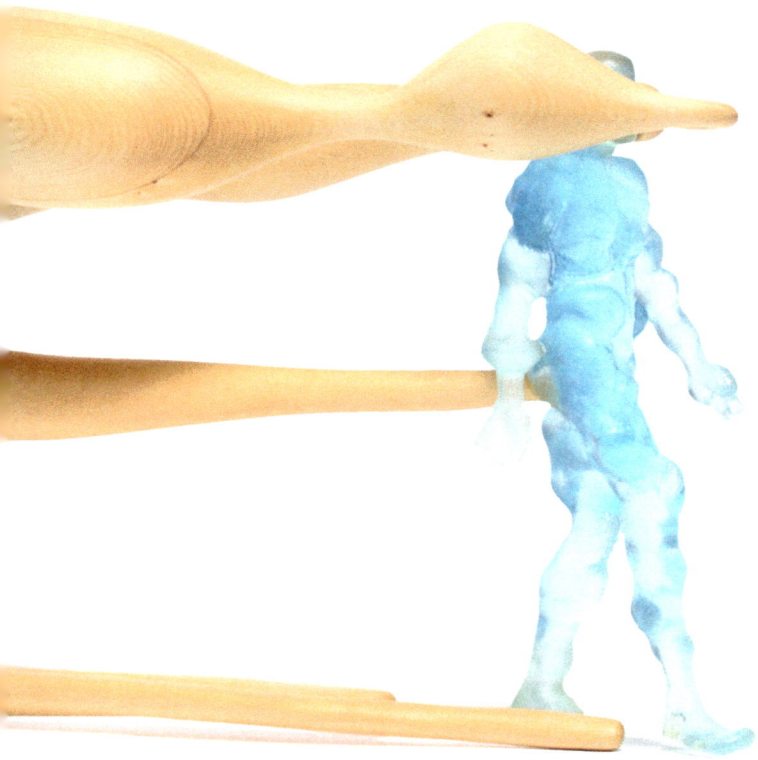

Seduce Me is a humorous yet scientifically accurate series of short films on the reproductive lives of animals. Actor and animal behaviour expert Isabella Rossellini embodies a different species in every episode. With the help of playful scenography and costuming, she acts out their wide-ranging mating rituals. She opens each episode with 'Is he seducing me? What am I, a...?', inviting us to take on – or at least imagine – a non-human perspective.

Isabella Rossellini, *Salmon* (left) and *Seahorse*, from the *Seduce Me* series, 2010

Julia Lohmann imagines a council of seaweed – a gathering of species she collected in Europe and East Asia. Set within a soundscape of the rising and falling tide, this installation offers a new perspective on coastal ecosystems. The enigmatic forms reveal seaweed's properties and potential as a design material, inviting connection on a human scale. If we consider that all living things have their own needs and agency, we might ask: what does seaweed think of us? How can we use this regenerative resource responsibly, meeting our own needs while learning to care for seaweed in return?

Julia Lohmann, *Kelp Council*, 2025

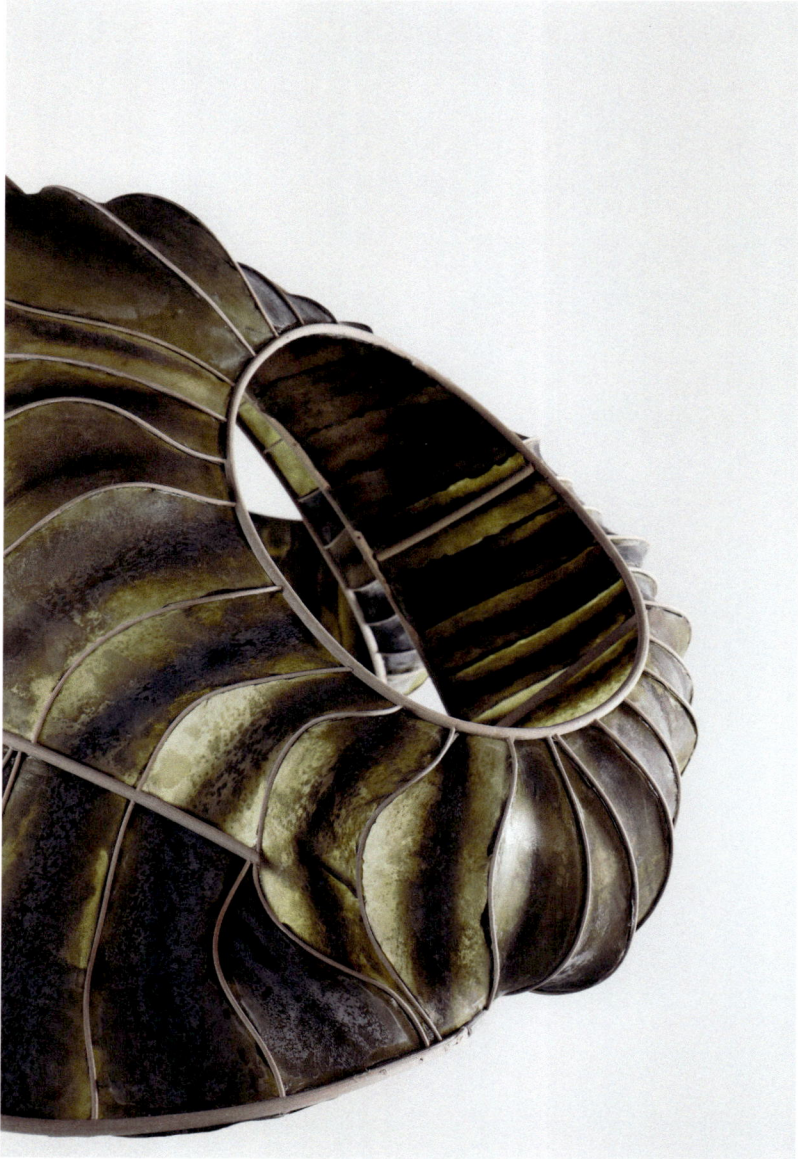

Julia Lohmann, details from *Kelp Council*, 2025

Alexandra Daisy Ginsberg, *Pollinator Pathmaker*, 2025

Can the audience for an artwork be more-than-human? Since 2021, Alexandra Daisy Ginsberg has been making art for pollinators, not about them. Her international project *Pollinator Pathmaker* presents a new approach to ecological action by creating art for the more-than-human world. Ginsberg developed a unique algorithmic tool that generates planting schemes optimised for pollinator diversity, rather than human aesthetics. These living artworks are then planted and cared for by humans. Her experiment in 'algorithmic altruism' asks whether we can embed alternative value systems in the technologies we make or if human creativity inherently prioritises our needs.

Pollinator Pathmaker began with the question: If pollinators designed gardens, what would humans see? Through the fellowship, Ginsberg developed a new iteration of the work based on a hypothetical relandscaping of the Design Museum site, radically prioritising its more-than-human visitors over human ones. She identified 1,400 square metres of the museum's forecourt that could be planted with a living artwork of thousands of pollinator-friendly plants. Designing the beds as if they would be planted, she then fed them into her *Pollinator Pathmaker* algorithmic tool, which generates unique planting schemes optimised for pollinators.

As a proposition towards manifesting this landscape, Ginsberg created an 8 metre-long tapestry to realise the work, drawing on the medium's history in art as a utopian space. The tapestry depicts the flowers and plants in 'pollinator vision', the artist's device to simulate how pollinators perceive colours differently from humans. Ginsberg also plays with the flora's scale to shrink human viewers to the size of pollinating insects. The viewer is invited in as if they were a foraging pollinator. The tapestry offers an alternative perspective on gardens, posing an aesthetic question: can an artwork help us experience the world of another species? And, if so, can it invite empathy for the more-than-human?

More than Human Fellow

Alexandra Daisy Ginsberg, detail of *Pollinator Pathmaker: Perceptual Field 7SzzLn6GnY97DSo7hCSLMf* tapestry, 2025

Detail of unrealised edition *7SzzLn6GnY97DSo7hCSLMf* in midsummer in human vision
Opposite: Detail of *7SzzLn6GnY97DSo7hCSLMf* in late summer in 'Pollinator Vision'

Alexandra Daisy Ginsberg, preparation sketch of *Pollinator Pathmaker: Perceptual Field 7SzzLn6GnY97DSo7hCSLMf*, 2025

Afterword

As a rule, creatures don't do progress. Generation follows generation along the trails, burrows and flightways of its predecessors. The direction of travel is always towards where ancestors have been before. That is why every way of life is also a way of remembering. Yet even as they go forth in life, creatures lean over those that follow behind, in a gesture of care and attention, even of love. Each generation, as we say colloquially, 'looks after' the next. Indeed, for most creatures, their life's work consists in creating the conditions for their offspring to flourish, sometimes in the most unpromising of environments. In this work, they often display much ingenuity, improvising makeshift arrangements that help them find their way around unexpected impediments as and when they crop up. If this is design, then it is a matter of muddling along, always in the midst of things, towards a future which, for those who have gone before, is already past.

Human beings, for most of their time on this earth, have done much the same. They too have muddled along, in tandem with the various non-human beings with which or whom they have shared their lives, in the same current of time, keeping their ancestors before and their descendants aft. We are used to calling their ways of life 'traditions' – a word derived from the Latin verb *tradere*, meaning 'to hand over' or 'to pass on', much as a baton in a relay race, thanks to which a coming generation can impart new energy to the life process even as the energy of forebears begins to wane. Yet unlike the race, the imperative of tradition is not to cross the finishing line but to keep on going.

Some three centuries ago, however, at the dawn of what we now know as the modern era, all this was set to change. A generation of thinkers, promising a new philosophy of Enlightenment, would denounce ancestral ways as backward. To progress in life, they said, meant crossing the line. Turning their backs not only on their own traditions, but also on the creaturely ways of non-human companions, this generation claimed the present for itself, and saw in the future a vision of a new world coming towards it, destined to replace the old. Its mission was to turn this vision into reality. It would do so by instigating a programme of design, to establish the universal principles on which the new order would rest, and of education, to train the next generation into compliance with it. With these programmes of design and education, a life's work would consist not in introducing new people into old ways but in building a world for them to occupy, and enforcing the conditions of their entry to it. For modern thinkers, with their targets set upon the future, the past would lie not ahead but behind. It was over, finished, a back-catalogue of forms of life, whether human or non-human, fated for conservation or extinction. It would hold no promise for times to come.

This turn on the past was bound to repeat itself. For as every subsequent generation came of age, it would follow suit by spurning the designs of its predecessors, only to project a new, allegedly superior design in their place. The effect was to set up a ratchet mechanism which, like clockwork, would notch up progress as a linear sequence of stoppages. With every design abandoned or superseded even before it is fully realised, to be replaced by the next, the upshot, compounded over generations, was an accumulating pile of debris. And it is this pile that confronts us today, clogging the lands and oceans of our planet. Should the accumulation continue unabated, it will sooner or later choke the Earth and its atmosphere, jeopardising the planet's very capacity to sustain life. Mitigating technologies designed to alleviate the worst effects of environmental degradation can offer only stopgap solutions, so long as the ratchet of progress is still in place. Recovery demands a fundamental change of direction.

It is as if we were in the driving seat of a car, accelerating down the fast lane of a highway. Mirrors on either side afford a rear view. Our metalled road, on which nothing grows, slices through a world threaded by a rhizomatic mesh of trails, roots and runners, as much aerial as earthly. Along these lines of life, since time immemorial, creatures of all sorts, including humans, have gone about their business. Animating this worldly tangle of more-than-human ways is a power to give birth to new life which the ancients knew as 'nature' (from the Latin *nascere*, 'to be born'). And to the peculiarly human task of looking after this new-borne life, so that it might grow and flourish, they gave the name 'culture' (from *colere*, 'to cultivate'). But for us, all this lies far behind. Is it then we, encapsulated in our vehicle, or they, denizens of the more-than-human world, who are heading for oblivion?

It is all a matter of perspective. Reflected in our rearview mirrors as we hurtle down the highway, we glimpse species of nature on one side, and traditions of culture on the other, both on the point of vanishing into the distance. Suppose however that we exchange the perspective from the driving seat for that of the inhabitants left by the roadside as we speed by. All at once, the fugitive reflections of nature and culture come back to life in a world that revolves around the comings and goings of the people themselves. It is they who hold the centre now, while we shoot off into the void. Only from this centre can they discharge their responsibility of care towards the manifold forms of life around them. What matters to them is nature's naturing, its continuous rebirth or natality. It is the work of culture, then, to look after what nature brings forth, rather than to preserve and catalogue its vestigial forms before they disappear.

Herein lies the change of perspective, to which Justin McGuirk refers in his introduction to this volume, from the major to the minor key. Resolutely

216

progressive, design in the major seeks to build a better world. Correcting what it regards as the mistakes of the past, it sees the future as a problem to be solved. Minor design, by contrast, is less problem-solving than problem-posing. It does not aspire to build back better, for the implied comparison – better versus worse – once again disowns the past in the name of progress. The good, in minor design, lies in the promise not of improvement but of recommencement. Its commitment is to the continuity of life. Opening a path to perfection rather than cutting it short with ready-made solutions, minor design feels its way tentatively into the future while honouring the ways of the past, along a path of renewal that knows no end. In the minor key, all designing is remembering. That's what it means to design both with and for a living, more-than-human world, and we have this exhibition to prove it.

Tim Ingold

Biographies

Jennifer Cunningham is a design researcher with a background in material culture. Based in Vienna she works as a researcher and Assistant Editor for Future Observatory and teaches research methods at design schools in Europe and North America. She has edited books with a focus on localised fabrication for designers and architects in Vienna, Zurich and Sweden.

Margherita Dosi Delfini is an Assistant Curator at the Design Museum, where she is currently working on the exhibition More than Human and previously helped deliver a retrospective of Enzo Mari. Margherita formerly held positions at Nicoletta Fiorucci Foundation and Barbican Art Gallery.

Anthony Dunne and Fiona Raby are partners in the design studio Dunne & Raby and University Professors of Design and Social Inquiry at Parsons/The New School in New York. Their projects and writing explore ways of bringing speculative thought from philosophy, science, and literature into conversation with design.

Daisy Hildyard is author of two novels – *Emergency* (2022) and *Hunters in the Snow* (2014) – and one work of nonfiction, *The Second Body* (2017). She lives in the north of England.

Tim Ingold is Professor Emeritus of Social Anthropology at the University of Aberdeen. His work extends from studies of peoples of the circumpolar North, through human ecology and evolutionary theory, to environmental perception, skilled practice and the relations between anthropology, art, architecture and design. In 2022, Ingold was made a CBE for services to Anthropology.

Andrés Jaque is a PhD architect. He is the founder of the Office for Political Innovation, and Dean and Professor of the Columbia University Graduate School of Architecture, Planning and Preservation.

Rebecca Lewin is a curator and writer focusing on the intersections of contemporary art, design and ecology. She is currently Senior Curator at the Design Museum, where she is co-curating the exhibition More than Human. She was previously Curator of Exhibitions and Design at the Serpentine Galleries, as well as producing independent exhibitions, publications and teaching internationally.

Anna Lowenhaupt Tsing is Distinguished Professor of Anthropology at the University of California, Santa Cruz. She is the author of *The Mushroom at the End of the World* (2015) and the co-author of *Field Guide to the Patchy Anthropocene* (2024). She is also a Professor at Aarhus University.

Justin McGuirk is the Director of Future Observatory, the Design Museum's national research programme for the green transition. He is also the former Chief Curator of the Design Museum. A writer and curator, he has produced numerous high-profile exhibitions and is the author or editor of ten books, including *Radical Cities* (2014) and *Ai Weiwei: Making Sense* (2023).

James Peplow Powell is an architect, more-than-human designer and co-founder of the research collective Feral Partnerships. He was Design Researcher in Residence at the Design Museum 2022-23, International Artist in Residence at Spreepark Berlin in 2024, and is an Associate Lecturer in Architecture at Sheffield Hallam University. His work explores the systemic and design implications of more-than-human interdependence.

Michelle Westerlaken is an interdisciplinary design researcher specialising in biodiversity technologies and multispecies design. She is currently an Impact Fellow at the Massachusetts Institute of Technology, previously a postdoctoral researcher at the University of Cambridge, with a PhD (2020) in Interaction Design from Malmö University.

Jia Yi Gu is an architectural historian, curator, and designer working on histories of knowledge production through the lens of media studies, cultural techniques and material cultures. Her projects explore changing definitions of architectural knowledge from the building site to the desktop. She is Assistant Professor of Architecture at Harvey Mudd College and co-director of Spinagu.

Index

Page numbers for images and
their captions are in *italic*.

221

Picture credits

Ordered by page number. Every reasonable attempt has been made to identify owners of copyright. Errors and omissions notified to the publisher will be corrected in subsequent editions. Abbreviations are: A – above, B – bottom, L – left, R – right.

Cover: Photo Daniel Mansur. Courtesy the artist and Mendes Wood DM, São Paulo, Brussels, Paris, New York; p. 5: Photo Daniel Mansur. Courtesy the artist and Mendes Wood DM, São Paulo, Brussels, Paris, New York; p. 15: Photo Fina Torres. Courtesy Ana Khan; p. 20: Photo Richard Round-Turner. © the Design Museum; p 24: © The Royal Society; p. 31: Drew Kelly for Future Observatory Journal; p. 33: Courtesy Anna Tsing; p. 37: Photo Isabella Matheus. Collection of the Pinacoteca de São Paulo. Donated by Patrons of Contemporary Art of the Pinacoteca de São Paulo 2021, through the Pinacoteca Art and Culture Association – APAC, 2021; pp. 38, 39: Photo Daniel Mansur. Courtesy the artist and Mendes Wood DM, São Paulo, Brussels, Paris, New York; pp. 40, 41: Courtesy the artist and Kate MacGarry, London. Copyright the artist. Photo Angus Mill; pp. 42, 43, 44–5: Photo Richard Round-Turner. © the Design Museum; pp. 46, 47: © Federico Borella and Michela Balboni; pp. 48, 49: © Jonathan Baldock. Courtesy the artist and Stephen Friedman Gallery. Photo Todd-White Art Photography; pp. 50, 51: Museum of English Rural Life, University of Reading; pp. 52, 53: Courtesy the artist, Galeria Abra Caracas and Cecilia Brunson Projects; pp. 54–5: © Forensic Architecture/Forensis, 2025; pp. 56, 57: Courtesy Ursula Biemann; pp. 59, 60–1: Courtesy César Rodríguez-Garavito/MOTH; p. 63: Photo Richard Wera Mirim; pp. 64, 65: Courtesy Paulo Tavares, studio autônoma; p. 68: Photo Richard Round-Turner. © the Design Museum; p. 73: Sipa USA/Alamy Stock Photo; p. 75: Photo Alex Goad. Courtesy Reef Design Lab; p. 76: Courtesy Studio Ossidiana; p. 83: Missouri Botanical Garden; p. 85: Photo José Hevia. Andrés Jaque/Office for Political Innovation in association with M-Marble Project; p. 87: Photo José Hevia. Andrés Jaque/Office for Political Innovation; p. 93: Photograph from *Automata: Artificial Figures of Men and Animals, History and Technique* by Alfred Chapuis and Edmond Droz, 1949; p. 95: Courtesy Bento Architecture; p. 98: © Pitt Rivers Museum, University of Oxford, 1960.6.3; p. 99: © Pitt Rivers Museum, University of Oxford, 1905.36.3; p. 100: Museum of English Rural Life, University of Reading; p. 101a: © Pitt Rivers Museum, University of Oxford, 1909.32.13.1; p. 101b: © Pitt Rivers Museum, University of Oxford, 1978.20.385; p. 102a: Museum of English Rural Life, University of Reading; p. 102b: © Pitt Rivers Museum, University of Oxford, 1931.66.31; p. 103: Museum of English Rural Life, University of Reading; pp. 104, 105: Courtesy Archivio Cesare Leonardi; p. 106al: © Pitt Rivers Museum, University of Oxford, 1958.3.35; p. 106ar: Museum of English Rural Life, University of Reading; p. 106bl: © Pitt Rivers Museum, University of Oxford, 1889.9.16; p. 106br: © Pitt Rivers Museum, University of Oxford, 1925.45.3; p. 107: Museum of English Rural Life, University of Reading; pp. 108, 109: Courtesy Canadian Centre for Architecture; pp. 110, 111: Photo Alex Goad. Courtesy Reef Design Lab; pp. 113, 114-5: Photo Ty Cole. Courtesy SCAPE; pp. 116, 117: Courtesy Weald to Waves; pp. 118, 119: Photo Maiju Suomi Courtesy Suomi/Koivisto Architects; p. 120: Photo Kyoungtae Kim. Courtesy Studio Ossidiana; p. 120ar: Photo Riccardo de Vecchi. Courtesy Studio Ossidiana; p. 121: Photo Kyoungtae Kim. Courtesy Studio Ossidiana; p. 122: Photo Bernardo Figueroa. Courtesy Marlène Huissoud; p. 123: Photo Chloe Bell. Courtesy Marlène Huissoud; pp. 124, 125: Photo Mikel Murizabal. Courtesy Andrés Jaque/Office for Political Innovation; p. 127: Photo Nicola Colella/Park Associati. Courtesy Studio Johanna Seelemann; pp 128, 129, 131: Photo Richard Round-Turner. © the Design Museum; pp. 132, 133: Courtesy SCAPE; pp. 134–5: © Corentin Mahieu × Bento × Sonian; pp. 136, 137: Dean Lever. Courtesy Jessie French &

Acknowledgements

This book was published in conjunction with the exhibition More than Human at the Design Museum, London, 11 July to 5 October 2025. The exhibition was curated by Justin McGuirk and Rebecca Lewin.

The exhibition and book were produced by Future Observatory, the Design Museum's national research programme for the green transition, in partnership with UKRI's Arts and Humanities Research Council.

We are grateful to the Miel de Botton Charitable Trust for supporting the exhibition.

Curators
Justin McGuirk
Rebecca Lewin

Assistant Curator
Margherita Dosi Delfini

Senior Exhibitions Project Manager
Gabria Lupone

Exhibitions Project Manager
Hannah Burgess
Elena Korotkikh

Exhibitions Coordinator
Madeleine Holley

Exhibition Graphic Design
Kellenberger–White

Exhibition Design
MSOMA Architects

The Design Museum owes its gratitude to all the lenders and organisations that contributed to the exhibition. Special thanks to colleagues and friends who have generously shared their knowledge and advice to aid the curatorial development of the exhibition. We are also grateful to Solange Pessoa for allowing us to use one of her works on the cover of the book.

In partnership with

the DESIGN MUSEUM

UKRI — Arts and Humanities Research Council

FUTURE OBSERVATORY

Imprint

Design Museum Publishing
224–228 Kensington High Street
London W8 6AG
United Kingdom

www.designmuseum.org
@designmuseum

First published in 2025
© 2025 Design Museum
Publishing

Publishing Manager
Stefano Mancin

Editor
Justin McGuirk

Assistant Editor
Jennifer Cunningham

Associate Editors
Rebecca Lewin
Margherita Dosi Delfini

Picture Editor
Anabel Navarro

Copyeditor
Simon Coppock

Proofreader
Elliot Hatt

Book Design
Kellenberger–White

KW Serif typeface and lettering
Kellenberger–White

Print and binding
robstolk®

Printed in The Netherlands

Distribution
Worldwide excluding USA
and Canada
Thames & Hudson
181A High Holborn
London WC1V 7QX
United Kingdom
www.thamesandhudson.com

USA and Canada
ARTBOOK | D.A.P
75 Broad Street, Suite 630
New York, NY10004
United States of America
www.artbook.com